Don't Tell'em You're Cold

"In Kathy Manley's memoir, she shows us how grinding poverty shaped her childhood, but her intelligence and determination ultimately defined her, allowing her to pay her strength forward to success for herself and her family."
— Phyllis Wilson Moore, literary historian, private researcher, author of the first official literary map of West Virginia

"*Don't Tell'em You're Cold* will simultaneously rip out your heart and cause you to cheer for the little girl who overcame the poverty she was born into. Her memoir gives us both a clear-eyed child's view of her family's hardships and her coming-of-age perseverance in overcoming them. If you think these times are behind us, her memoir should serve as a window into the life too many children still face today."
— Carter Taylor Seaton, author of *Hippie Homesteaders*

"An evocative, inspirational journey from grinding poverty to education, career and marriage, *Don't Tell'em You're Cold* is rich in its portrayal of place, time and personal relationships. In the early 1960s, as the so-called War on Poverty exposed the living conditions of Appalachia to the nation, Kathy struggles to help her family make ends meet. With her disabled father, she scavenges for coal and scrap iron, picks berries, begs in coal camps and outside the five and dime, and dreams of having toys and clothes like other children. Inside the family's rough home, where free calendars and pictures of the baby Jesus cover cracks in the walls, she cooks, cleans, defrosts water pipes, chases out the roaches and asks God why her mother ran off. Manley writes in a refreshingly matter-of-fact, unsentimental way, with an engaging, self-effacing wit. Poverty is certainly no joke, but the fact that Manley finds humor in even the most dire situations points to her strength of spirit."
— David Mould, author of *Monsoon Postcards: India Ocean Journeys*

"Kathy Manley's vividly detailed memoir takes us inside her 6-year-old self, sliding down into a county dump, past the rats that scuttle in and out of the fetid garbage, in order to reach just the right piece of wood her father needs for a new peg leg. We see her as a ninth grader after her mother abandons the family when it's up to her to keep her two younger siblings fed, clean, and clothed. As Manley's memories unfold, a portrait is painted of a determined woman who must reach deep into herself for the faith and strength to not just endure but to prevail."
— Anna Smucker, author of *Rowing Home*

"Long after you finish Kathy Manley's book, you'll hold onto the hope that undergirds her memoir, a hope Manley learned from her father and his search for the perfect wooden leg, a hope that comes through in Manley's great, buoyant spirit that carries us through to the last page and beyond. Ride The Blue Goose and read this fine book."
— Jim Minick, Author of *Fire Is Your Water: A Novel* and *The Blueberry Years: A Memoir of Farm and Family*

"This richly reflective memoir is sure to be a superlative addition to the Mountain State Press list of books highlighting the real experiences of the people of West Virginia. Manley's poignant memories of a childhood spent in poverty are told with a plain spoken, appropriate candor and so create a memoir whose boundaries are uniquely Manley's own. With every anecdote can be observed the rich resilience of a human soul refusing to surrender to either self-pity or resignation, an achievement I can only admire and respect."
— Marc Harshman, Poet Laureate of West Virginia

Don't Tell 'em You're Cold

A MEMOIR OF POVERTY AND RESILIENCE

KATHERINE P. MANLEY

Copyright 2019 by Katherine P. Manley
All rights reserved.

First edition published by Mountain State Press, Inc.
Printed in the United States of America

No part of this book may be reprinted without the express permission of the author and publisher, except for excerpts for reviews and according to fair use laws in the classroom.

ISBN: 9781687572318

The following chapters, or a version of them, were previously published:
"Radioland" first appeared in *Hamilton Stone Review*
"Bubble Gum Man" first appeared in *Traditions: A Journal of West Virginia Folk Culture and Educational Awareness*
"Poverty Brain" first appeared in a similar version in *Fearless: Women's Journeys to Self-Empowerment*

Edited by Cat Pleska
Line Editor: Michele Schiavone
Cover photo by Rex, courtesy of the author
All other photos courtesy of the author

MOUNTAINSTATEPRESS.ORG

Scott Depot, West Virginia

ACKNOWLEDGMENTS

I thank God for giving me strength and wisdom to overcome the many challenges I experienced as a child and the numerous blessings he continuously bestows. Among those blessings are the following people who stood by me and helped this book become a reality. I would like to share this awesome writing journey with you that God put me on.

First of all, I owe a debt of gratitude to Dr. Fran Simone, director of the 1995 West Virginia Writing Project, who first recognized the value of my work and gave me the vision. She suggested I attend Hindman Appalachian Writers Workshop in Kentucky where I had the pleasure of having Lee Smith and husband Hal Crowther as mentors. Their critiques gave me further confidence to continue writing.

The next summer I attended Chautauqua Writers Workshop in New York and met mentors Kent Brown, Peter Jacobi, and Dayton Hyde, who further instilled in me the need to keep my rear in the chair and get the book written. I promised them and myself that I would write during the summer when I wasn't teaching. Believe me, it took several summers.

During this time, I also became a member of West Virginia Writers and attended their annual June conference in Cedar Lakes, West Virginia. I became friends with several talented writers who took time to listen to my stories, read them, and offer valuable advice. Warm appreciation to Sandy Tritt, Rhonda Browning, Kate Long, Phyllis Wilson Moore, Cat Pleska, Meredith Sue Willis, Michael Knost, Kirk Judd, Marc Harshman, Anna Smucker, and Cheryl Ware for their enthusiastic support and encouragement.

Also, warm regards to the late Dennis Deitz, Charleston, WV, who called me frequently and invited me to Bob Evans to share sausage sandwiches and talk about my book. Our meetings kept me motivated and determined.

Many thanks to the Charleston Memoir Writers for all the advice and support during our monthly meetings. Fran and David, you helped me grow as a writer and stay on track. Thank you for your belief in my story and in my ability to write it.

Many thanks to my family and friends who frequently asked, "How's the book coming along?" The interest you showed kept me motivated to get it done.

To the families and childhood friends who lived in the #16 Island Creek Coal Camp at Verdunville, know that I will never forget the memories we made in and around our very special neighborhood. To my neighbor Lois June who gave me my first donut, taught me how to mash potatoes, and always saved a cup of Thanksgiving punch for me; to Kathleen who took time to pat me on the head and tell me I was a pretty little girl when she came to the store to shop along with her several children. To Betty and Olive, clerks at the store, who were patient and allowed me to take all the time I needed to trade an empty pop bottle for three cents' worth of candy. Your kindness and camaraderie will never be forgotten. In a great way, you helped me get through those difficult teenage years.

I also want to acknowledge my husband, David, who listened to first drafts and laughed and cried with me. Also, for tirelessly sharing this journey with me—helping me remember by driving me to the river, searching for sprawling blackberry bushes, and doing anything else I asked him to do.

Finally, I cannot thank Cat Pleska enough for her belief in me and her considerable skills in getting my story where it needed to be. I sincerely appreciate her efforts and all that she has done.

DEDICATION

To the memory of my father
John West Evans
1911–1976

who raised me never to quit
and taught me how to dream.

and

To the memory of my mother
Rosa Casey Evans
1930–1984

who told us stories and sang to us—
she tried, but couldn't hold on

CONTENTS

Introduction	10
Daddy's Leg	12
Turn This Way	20
The Blue Goose	29
Treasures Along the Mile	36
First Ride	39
Duz or Breeze?	42
First Year in School	46
Moving Day	54
Our New House	57
Bean Days	63
Starting Over	64
City Sidewalks	73
Christmas	80
Winter of 1960	84
Democrat Rally	91
Entertainment	95
Black Gold	101
Mommy	108
The Best of 1960	109
Relatives	112
Saturday Morning Line-up	119
Bubble Gum Man	121
Survivor	124
6JE6	130
Bend of the River	136
A Quarter and a Penny	140
Coal Camp Beatles	146
Radio Land	150
Trick-or-Treat	156
Prayer Time	164

Winter Morning	165
Growing Up	169
Thirteen	170
Where's Mommy?	174
American Bandstand	175
Decorating	182
It Will Be Good for You	184
A Letter from Mommy	188
All Men Are Not Created Equal	190
Dancing And Dating	193
Juggling It All	200
Senior Year	207
Graduation Day	212
Moving On	215
Priorities	218
Engagement	224
Wedding Day	230
Nothing Remains the Same	236
Big Ben	239
Epilogue: Fingertips	242

INTRODUCTION

Poverty never seems to leave any society. Each day, we hear of a group somewhere in the world who suffers hunger, lack of housing and medical care, deprivations of all kinds. To most of us, it is a news story, and even though we are spurred to action sometimes with donations to different organizations, we usually have only a vague idea of what poverty is like for the individual, especially a child.

In *Don't Tell'em You're Cold*, we get an extreme close-up of poverty: poverty of place, of family, of the individual. Kathy's stories begin in mid twentieth century and through to the changing decades of the 60s and 70s until she triumphed through perseverance and hard work and was poor no more. No one should shut their eyes to what many had to live with and through, and this memoir creates vivid details of how poverty always looks. When you read this story, any rhetoric about freeloaders or lazy people of little means should vanish in the harsh light of the author's reality. Families fall through the cracks and forces beyond their control can shape and guide each person and their circumstances.

Manley's father is but one example of how falling through the cracks of safety results in destitution. How does a man with severe disabilities provide for his family? Manley shows us his determined resolve to tap whatever resources he can find, even if it's his own six-year-old daughter rummaging in the dump for an appropriate piece of wood to carve for his peg leg. At other times, it meant she helped him gather loose pieces of coal that fell from the tipple or in the broiling heat of summer she'd don a double-layer of clothing to go blackberry picking, aided by a stick for scaring snakes away. She even helped him beg on the streets in frigid weather, yet her father never failed to make her aware of others less fortunate. Gratitude is not a virtue many people think the poor possess, but of course they do.

All through *Don't Tell'em You're Cold*, no matter the challenge, Manley intuitively managed to not only survive but also to cope with the stress, and her developing fortitude is amazing. Like any child, however, she clung to the fun moments and good times, and naturally had a wish for a toy or two. She was, after all, just a little girl. Swept along with the tide of survival as she comes of age, the outer world reached her small community, and she comes to love the Beatles and longs for a time when she has more than the barest essentials for life. Manley's close relationship with her father helped forge a commitment by her to her whole family, even though not all members were as strong.

Manley's memoir reveals that grinding poverty need not always create failure and despair. Sometimes hope rests in the small, dirty faces of children such as she, who grew up to set goals and to answer the needs of her parents and herself. Manley reveled in the support of her teachers, who were heroes to her. She grew up to become one of the most awarded educators in her state, and in the country. Her story opens our minds to the possibility that we'll do more than donate to Goodwill, and perhaps we will encourage a child and help them move beyond circumstances to success. Maybe we'll also open our hearts to the reality of what it means to be poor, to the truth of what every child needs: a sound home, good food, medical care, an education, a job, and dreams that have the best chance to come true.

Cat Pleska, editor

Daddy's Leg

I bounced on the edge of the truck seat, ready to help Daddy switch gears. We were headed to the dump in our 1948 Chevy panel truck. Years earlier, Sunbeam Bakery used it to deliver breads and cakes, but although it was rusted from front to back, it worked for us.

Daddy's old, wooden peg leg was worn out, and he needed materials to make a new one. If I was lucky, I might also discover a treasure just for me. I was six that summer of 1958, and there was nothing I loved better than to go scouting in the dump with Daddy.

"Not just any piece of wood will do," Daddy said. "It has to be long and thick. We'll have to look at it carefully, to make sure it won't splinter."

"Okay, Daddy." He was like that. He always took time to explain things to me.

Minutes before, I had waved goodbye to Mommy as she stuffed clothes into the Maytag washer. Margaret Ann, my one-year-old sister, played nearby on the porch of our two-room house. At the end of the holler, Daddy turned left on Paint Creek Road toward Charleston, West Virginia, where the dump was located. We drove along Paint Creek quite a while, and I noticed clusters of houses here and there.

I was born in our house at Holly Grove, the only house I knew by that time. Paint Creek flowed between two mountains and ran alongside the curvy hardtop. We passed by the two-room school that sat in the bottom land behind the houses. In a couple of months, I would enter school there as a first grader. I couldn't wait.

Daddy spoke and drew my attention from looking out the window as he continued his instructions about the leg. "Now when you go looking through the tires, keep your eyes peeled for one that's not bald. It needs good tread for the end of the leg." He scratched his scruffy chin and shifted gears. The truck jerked against the ruts in the dirt road leading to the county dump.

I hoped we could find what Daddy needed, so he wouldn't have to use crutches. They rubbed under his arms and made them sore. I started looking for wood the second he turned off the main road.

Daddy had lost his right leg at sixteen, when he tried to hop a train bound for Kentucky, he'd told me. A few years later, he lost most of his left hand when he was unloading cases of dynamite at a coal company. After the explosion, his little finger and a nub of thumb were all he had left. Somehow, he ended up on Paint Creek doing odd jobs, and that's where he met and married Mommy in 1950, almost eight years before. I knew the stories well.

Daddy slowed the truck—we'd named her *The Blue Goose*—to a crawl, and I pressed my nose against the window to peer out at the piles of junk scattered on the side of the road leading through the dump. "That sofa looks good," I said.

He shielded his eyes from the sun's glare with his half-hand. "No, it doesn't. It's broken in the middle and springs are poking out everywhere."

We crept past rusted washing tubs and broken kitchen tables. Coils of cable and stacks of stained metal covered the ground as far as we could see. Nothing interested Daddy enough to make him stop, so we pushed up the mountain to the head of the dump.

The Blue Goose lurched around and through stacks of abandoned furniture, piles of broken toys, and bags of garbage. Daddy studied the raggedy stacks of logging timbers, searching for a good slab of wood. After a bit, his eyebrows shot upward. He'd spotted something. He shut off Goose's motor. We got out and poked through the pile of wood, and I pulled out a long, narrow board and knocked off the sawdust. I held it up so he could see.

He shook his head. "Keep looking, Kathy. That's not wide enough."

"How about that one?" I pointed to a rough piece of lumber that was wider than the first board, but not as tall as I was. I tried to lift it, but it was too heavy.

Daddy picked it up and turned it around, examining it. "No, it's sycamore. See those knots running through? My saw can't cut through 'em."

Nothing was quite right. Every piece had a split or hard knots. It was already hot and sticky. I swatted away gnats and wiped sweat from my forehead. This was taking longer than I'd thought, and I still hadn't been able to search for my own treasure.

I turned when Daddy grunted. He'd found a piece about four feet long and a foot wide. He pulled it closer with one of his crutches, studied it and picked it up.

"I believe this white pine will do." He hefted it in his good hand. "It's light and sturdy." We loaded it into the truck. "Keep watching," he said, as he started the engine. "We might get lucky and find a tire laying right here."

We drove around the dump twice, but didn't get lucky. Not a single tire anywhere. We drove to the top of the dump and looked over the edge. I peered at the garbage below. At the very bottom lay several black donuts. "Down there, Daddy."

He leaned over me, stared at the dark heap, and nodded. "You're gonna have to go down there and get one."

The dump stank of soured garbage. Rats scampered in and out of torn trash bags, and rotting food was scattered everywhere. As I started down the hill, a large rat darted into the end of an old pipe lying in front of me. I took a step backward and looked up at Daddy. That thing scared me.

"Go on. It won't hurt you. It's hiding over there. You can climb down the other side." He pointed to a pair of old bedsprings partly covered with broken sheetrock. I scooted across the bedspring onto a piece of old carpet. I moved carefully between pieces of slippery linoleum and slick tarpaper. It was as if I were sledding in winter. The only thing worse than sliding to the bottom was the awful smell.

Still, as I made my way down the garbage pile, I kept my eyes open for a special treasure. A doll, maybe, or a jump rope. Something I could keep and play with. Anything.

Finally, I reached the tires. I turned over two or three, but they had large gashes. One had a nest of some sort within it, and another had huge water bugs climbing in and out. I kept looking until I spotted one lying under an old kitchen cabinet.

"I think I found one," I yelled to Daddy.

"Check it good," he said. "Make sure it's not worn."

I inspected the tire. "Looks pretty good to me. Want me to bring it up?"

"If you can," he said.

I slipped my hands inside the rim of the tire and tugged, but the wooden cabinet pinned it to the ground. I sat down, dug in my heels, gripped the tire, and pulled. It didn't budge. I kicked the stupid cabinet. Determined, I stood, dusted off my grimy hands, and leaned every ounce of my forty-something pounds into the cabinet, pushing and shoving until it finally gave in and rolled away. My back felt stiff when I straightened, and I turned to look up the hill, checking for the best path to climb with the tire.

Daddy pointed out what appeared to be the easiest route. He stood at the top and instructed me as I dragged the tire past rusty pipes, broken glass, and empty paint buckets. I pushed for a while, and I'd pull for a while. Finally, that tire and I made it to the top.

Daddy bent and looked at it. "You done good." He patted my shoulder. "Let's get it loaded." I rolled it to the back of the truck and helped him throw it in.

We climbed into the truck, and Daddy slid his crutches behind the seat. I grabbed the wooden sticks I used to help Daddy drive sometimes. He pumped the gas hard three times, held the pedal down with his good left leg and turned the key.

The engine struggled to turn over and failed. Daddy repeated the steps twice more, and at last the engine caught. The Blue Goose screeched and squawked to life.

"Get ready," he said.

I knew what to do. I put the sticks in position: gear stick on my lap, clutch stick in my left hand, and gas stick in my right. He revved up the engine, and I got the gas stick ready.

"All right, give it gas," he ordered. I leaned over and gently pressed the gas pedal with the gas stick. Daddy switched his good foot to the clutch. Our timing had to be perfect.

"A little harder," he said.

I pushed down on the gas stick, and Daddy eased up on the clutch. The truck lurched forward, and I grinned. Daddy didn't always need me to help drive. He steered the truck with his pinky finger on his half-palm, pressed the clutch with his good left leg and punched the gas pedal with his stick. I helped whenever I could, especially on the rutted roads, like the one leading to the dump.

Driving down the mountain, we spotted a green sofa cushion sitting in a mud puddle. One end looked good enough to use. Daddy pulled the truck over and turned off the motor, and we jumped out. I tossed it into the back of the truck. My shoulders drooped as I scanned the area, seeing little more than more garbage and junk. No treasure. I was happy I could help Daddy, but I had hoped I could find something for me, too.

I squinted into the sun, wishing something special would appear, would catch my eye. I turned to head back to the truck, and out of the corner of my eye, I saw it. I saw *him*.

I gasped and put my filthy hand over my mouth. "Daddy!" I pointed to where the clock sat, partially covered by a feed sack. "It's Big Ben!" Before my Daddy could respond, I hurdled a black garbage bag, a broken cinderblock, and a rusted metal bucket, and I knelt before Big Ben. This—*this* was the treasure I'd hoped for.

I pushed away the rotting burlap sack, brushed mud off the metal clock, and lifted it onto my lap. The metal statue was in the shape of a man—Big Ben, I was sure—because Mommy and Daddy called the alarm clock at home Big Ben. He held a strange wheel that had sticks coming out of it, and a broken clock face was centered in the wheel. The man wore a suit and beneath him were carved words I couldn't read.

"Roosevelt," Daddy said from behind me. "That's a Roosevelt clock. That man is President Franklin Delano Roosevelt. He was President of the United States a few years back. "Nice find, Kathy."

"I thought his name was Big Ben like our clock at home."

Daddy chuckled. "No. Big Ben is the name of a clock *tower*, not a man. It's at a big palace in London."

"What's a palace?"

"Like a castle."

I thought about that for a minute. "Can I go see Big Ben and the castle?"

Daddy looked away, and that bright sun must have made his eyes water, because he was wiping them dry when he turned back to me. "Someday, Kathy, when you get older, I want you to go see Big Ben. See for yourself what that clock looks like." He dusted off his gray work pants. "Nothing in this world would make me happier."

I used my shirt to rub off the dirt from the clock statue's head. I held the clock to my chest and squeezed it. I didn't care who called him president or who called him Dohickey Rosey-whatever. To me, he was, and would always be, Big Ben.

With our shopping trip complete, Daddy and I climbed into The Blue Goose and headed home, Big Ben carefully wedged on the floorboard between my feet.

Daddy backed close to the hillside beside our house. He and Mommy built it right after they got married in September. It had a kitchen, bedroom, and porch made from rough lumber. They just had finished when the first snowflake dropped from the sky. The gray boards were wide with gaps in between. A huge coal pile stood beside the house along with his junk pile. Mommy came out to meet us after Daddy parked. "Did you buy flour?" she asked.

Daddy opened the back doors to the truck and began unloading. "No, we went to the dump today. We'll tackle that tomorrow."

She sighed. "I can't make bread without flour," she said. "There's beans on the stove." She turned without another word and walked into the house, not waiting to see what we'd found.

That night, Daddy let me stay up late to watch him sculpt the dump wood into a brand new peg leg. He cut a patch of tire rubber about the size of a napkin with a knife and nailed it to the end of the leg to cushion his walk and prevent him from sliding. I held the screws for him as he mounted two metal belt braces on the top and middle that would fasten the leg to his waist. When he finished that, he cut a small section of the green sofa cushion and used it for a kneepad.

Daddy stood the leg upright and put the pad in position. He centered his knee on the pad, threaded a long belt through the top brace, and buckled it. He strapped a smaller belt around his leg near the knee. The two belts held the wooden leg in place.

I held my breath as Daddy tried it out. He walked around the kitchen table, stopping occasionally to adjust one of the belts or reposition the kneepad. "It'll do," he said. He picked up Margaret Ann and sat her on the back of his leg stump. She wrapped her arms around his leg and held on as he rode her around the kitchen table. She laughed as the leg shook and swung in different directions. For a second, I wished that I was that little again, so I could ride on Daddy's leg.

Mommy smiled as Margaret rode around the table and after three or four times, she lifted her off. "Bedtime," she said. Margaret wasn't finished riding and reached out for the leg, but Mommy carried her into the bedroom anyway. In a few minutes I heard Mommy's soft voice half singing-half humming.

Daddy picked up his tools and turned to smile at me. "Now you'd better get in bed. Tomorrow, we've got to get a load of coal."

I wiped my face and hands at the sink, slipped into a clean shirt, and went into the bedroom. There were two iron beds—one against each wall—and a pot-bellied stove in between. Mommy and Margaret Ann slept in one bed, and I slept at the foot of the bed on the other side and Daddy slept at the top.

I held Big Ben to my chest and carried him into bed, snuggling my prize, and fell asleep thinking of the day I'd see the real Big Ben in his castle.

Turn This Way

When Mommy got up, I did too. I decided Big Ben couldn't sleep in the bed anymore because his metal statue was too cold, so I stood him on the floor at the end of the bed. I'd have to think about finding him a better spot. I planned to clean him up when I got home from helping Daddy gather coal.

I followed Mommy into the kitchen in case she had any empty cans to throw away. I watched as she opened the side door on the cast iron stove and shoved in crumpled paper. She added small pieces of kindling and struck a match. She blew on the flames until they caught, adding in larger pieces of wood. Sometimes she threw in a small lump of coal or two to make the fire last, especially on days she cooked beans. Within a few minutes, the stove was hot and ready.

"You makin' gravy?" I whispered, trying not to wake Daddy or Margaret. I opened the refrigerator. "I'll get the milk."

"No gravy this morning—there's no flour." She poured water into a pot and placed it on a hot burner.

That meant no empty milk can, which I liked to play with. Mommy punched a hole in the top and when it was empty I'd fill it up with water from the creek. It looked like a real can of milk sitting on my make believe kitchen table. I'd be sure to remind Daddy to get flour so I could get an empty can.

The stove sat in one corner of the kitchen, a few feet from the wall. This is where I took a bath. I stood in the center of a small wash tub while Mommy soaped and rinsed me. And this is where I first heard the *hamburger story*. As she poured pots of rinse water on my shoulders, I turned around several times to make sure she rinsed away all the suds. And every time she saw that large brown mole on my upper thigh, she always said, "There's my hamburger! I craved hamburger before you were born, but I never got any. You've been marked." I didn't know what she meant by *being marked*, but I always giggled when she said that.

I wished Mommy would use the larger wash tub she washed clothes in. I wanted deeper water to play in after my bath. But she said the big tub took up too much room, used too much water, and was hard to carry through the door. In between baths, I wiped my face, hands, and legs with a washcloth before going to bed.

Mommy's grease can sat on the back side of the stove. She saved every drop of grease left over from anything fried including bacon, hamburger, fried potatoes, and eggs; Mommy re-used the grease for every meal to save on buying lard. Whenever it stunk, she emptied it and started saving grease again.

Buckets of coal and kindling sat on both sides of the stove, and larger pieces of wood lay behind it along with a few larger lumps of coal. Daddy busted those lumps into smaller pieces as needed. A large stovepipe rose from the top of the stove toward the ceiling and on through the roof. Heat from the stove felt good even on a June morning. Sometimes, when the stove got too hot, Mommy opened the kitchen door a little.

"Tell your Daddy to come and eat. It's 6 o'clock and ya'll need to get going."

I went to the bedroom, but he was awake and sitting on the edge of the bed. "I'm coming," he whispered. Margaret Ann was asleep with Mommy's pillow scotched by her side, so she wouldn't roll off the high iron bed. When I wasn't helping Daddy, I liked to play with her, and she always laughed when we played patty-cake and peek-a-boo.

I returned to the kitchen and watched Mommy spoon oats into the bowls. She replaced the pot on the stove but poured two cups of coffee for Daddy and herself before sitting down. Daddy stepped into the kitchen and finished buckling his leg belts. He pulled out a chair, bent over a little, and sat down, resting his wooden peg leg on the floor. He wore a slip-on shoe on his left foot, and the same gray shirt and pants from yesterday. Daddy only had two outfits, but none of us had very many clothes. Only what the corner rod in the bedroom held.

Mommy sipped her coffee. "John, tomorrow you need to change clothes and let me wash those." Daddy nodded. Mommy washed clothes on the front porch in a Maytag wringer washer. She rinsed them in a large aluminum wash tub and hung them to dry on a clothesline strung on the porch.

As we ate, I studied Mommy and Daddy. She had the prettiest black wavy hair I had ever seen and dark brown eyes. Daddy said she took after her Italian daddy, except she didn't have a handlebar mustache. Every time I imagined Mommy with a mustache, I laughed. But Mommy got her musical talent from him. She told me he sang every day and played his accordion that he brought from Sicily. She taught herself to play the guitar and she yodeled good, too. She played almost any song anyone named, and if she didn't know it, she learned it in no time.

Daddy had blue eyes and brown hair. Mommy said Daddy looked exactly like his mother from Eastern Kentucky. Margaret Ann and I took a little from each of them. We had brown eyes and brown hair. He played guitar, too, but different from Mommy. He laid it on his lap, picked the strings with his good hand, and slid a Sears metal socket from a socket wrench set across the other end with his half-hand.

While Daddy and I finished eating, Mommy poured water into an aluminum dish pan and placed it on the stove. She sprinkled powdered laundry detergent from a box into the water and swished it with her hands. This is the same soap box she used to wash our clothes with, too. Within seconds white suds floated on top waiting for our bowls and spoons. She rinsed the coffee pot and turned it upside down to drain. The only time I saw Mommy sit down was when she was eating or playing her guitar. She was always busy doing something around the house.

Finished eating, Daddy fastened his peg leg and headed toward the door. I slipped on my shoes and followed him. He stopped, tightened his leg and waist belts and continued toward the four steps leading to the yard. Mommy stood at the door and watched. "Be careful," she said. "Don't forget to bring home flour."

I nodded.

"Let me go down first," he said. "I need to see how this leg takes those steps." I backed up to give him plenty of room.

He grabbed a post for support and lifted the leg to the side. He lowered it onto the first step and stepped down with his good foot. He eased onto the second, third, and finally the fourth. Once on the dirt, he took a few steps back and forth and tugged on the knee pad. "It's heavier than the other leg, but I'll get used to it." He smiled. "Let's load up." I was happy that Daddy could walk on his new leg.

The Blue Goose started on the second try, and we rocked and rolled through the ruts. We turned left onto Paint Creek Road, drove to Hansford and crossed the Kanawha River and turned right toward the coal mines. Soon Daddy pulled up to the coal tipple.

Daddy and I knew the routine well. At 7:00 a.m. we sat in the cool morning air and waited patiently for our turn. "No use to get in a hurry," Daddy always said.

Black coal dust flew around us and sparkled in the early sunlight, making it hard to see anything. Still, no one could miss the large tin tipple, a building supported by huge wooden posts. The conveyor belt carrying the coal to the tipple stretched up the mountain like a huge slicky slide. The belt, about forty feet long and three feet wide, carried coal to trucks waiting at its end. On the front end of the tipple, a long set of steps led to a tiny booth where a man they called *the loader* operated the switches controlling the conveyor belt.

From his window, the loader watched how much coal dumped into each truck. "Don't go yet," he yelled and signaled to a coal-truck driver. "It'll hold some more." The trucker nodded and waited as the conveyor belt started up again, dumping football-sized lumps of coal into the truck bed.

"Remember, now, wait till that belt completely shuts off before you get out," Daddy said. "Then work fast."

"Okay."

"Don't ever stand under that belt, Kathy. It could turn on at any time. Accidents happen." Daddy and I had been loading coal at the tipple ever since I was big enough to pick up a lump, but he said that every time.

The man in the tin booth peered hard out his window and watched as the last lumps of coal fell into the truck bed. He didn't cut the switch in time, and a few lumps fell off the truck and onto the ground.

"Wow!" I said. "Did you see that?"

Daddy smiled. I counted five big lumps.

The man in the booth waved his hand at the driver, and the truck pulled away and disappeared around the curve. As the truck passed, a heavy cloud of coal dust settled over The Blue Goose. The next driver pulled into position, and we waited for dumping to begin. The second truck filled, then the third, fourth, and fifth. The company had five trucks, and after what seemed to me like hours of waiting, all five trucks had loaded and left the hill. I'm not sure where they took the coal, but it wouldn't be long before they returned.

"It's almost our turn," Daddy said. I fidgeted with my driving sticks and jittered my foot against the floorboard. I couldn't wait to get out of the truck.

"Any second now. Wait for the signal."

After the roadway cleared, the tipple worker signaled us to come closer. We left our spot near the shed and pulled under the tipple. Lumps lay on the ground, in the ditch, and over the hill.

Daddy got out, opened the back doors, and removed the shovel. While he scooped up two or three lumps at a time, I searched for runaway lumps. We worked quickly, knowing that soon more coal trucks would come, and we'd have to quit scavenging.

As we loaded the last lump, loud engines roared up the mountain. "They're coming back," I yelled.

Daddy awkwardly climbed into The Blue Goose and backed out of the way. A few seconds later, all five trucks roared by, turned around at the end of the road, and lined up for another load.

"We did pretty good," I said. "About twenty lumps. After we sell it, we can go to the store for Mommy."

Daddy smiled, and I puffed out my chest and grinned back at him. In my family, we were expected to work, and I didn't want to let Daddy down.

The booth worker turned levers and pressed buttons. The noisy conveyor belt dumped more coal into each truck. The loaded trucks headed down the mountain once more to dump their coal. Again, we pulled under the tipple and loaded stray lumps of coal into The Blue Goose. This time, I searched farther from the truck, seeking rollaway lumps. I found a few on the side of the road near some bushes.

Daddy looked over the hill. "Come here," he said. "There's some overnighters down there." He called big lumps *overnighters* because they were large enough to burn all night in the stove. I climbed down the hill to get them and rolled the big lumps to the top and to the back of the truck. I helped Daddy heft the heavy ones.

After a few hours, the man in the tin booth blew the lunch whistle, and the hustle and bustle stopped. Drivers climbed out of their trucks, carrying brown paper bags. If it rained, they ate in their trucks, their windows rolled down and doors propped open. I'd listen while they talked to each other about family and work. That June day it was warm and sunny, so they settled under the trees beside the shed where Daddy and I parked. We waited in the truck.

Daddy tapped the little finger of his bad hand on the steering wheel. "I don't like this downtime," he said. "It delays us an hour."

I secretly liked it, because I waited for my lunch to come to me. Near the end of lunch hour, when the drivers finished eating, they shared treats with me. Sometimes, I got a ten-cent can of potted meat and four or five saltine crackers. One day I got a Mallo Cup candy bar. The driver told me to save the card inside, and I could get free candy, but he didn't tell me how. I saved it anyway.

One day, a driver offered me the rest of his Bubble-Up Soda. Daddy's nod said I could have it. This day, one driver handed me a half of a peanut butter sandwich and another gave me a store-bought cookie. I offered Daddy half of my half sandwich, but he told me to eat it. I never understood how Daddy could eat breakfast and go all day without eating again until late evening.

The whistle blew, and the coal tipple started up again. Coal flew out of the mountain on the long, narrow belt and hit hard in the back of the first truck. Soon that truck was loaded, and another one moved in to take its place. After several more hours, the last truck was filled, the belt stopped, and the mountain was silent.

We loaded The Blue Goose with every chunk of scrap coal we could find. Daddy threw the shovel on top of the coal and shut the back doors. I climbed inside and sat in my bucket seat beside him. He tugged on the large piece of plywood he put behind our seats, making sure it was secure. It prevented lumps of coal from rolling forward on us. He climbed in and started the motor, and I was glad it caught on the first try. I was tired.

Daddy drove down the mountain. In a few minutes, we were on the hard road. In my chest, my heart ticked faster, and the sticky clump in my throat felt familiar to me. I tried to swallow it down, but it wouldn't go. I breathed slowly, trying to make my heart act normal.

How many times had I asked Daddy? Each time, he'd say *no,* but not always in words. Sometimes he'd say it with his silence and that hurt me even more. I wondered if maybe it didn't hurt him, too. I squeezed shut my eyes and prayed to God that this time I would get lucky. Maybe, just maybe, Daddy would say *yes.*

At the end of the holler, we stopped at the intersection, and there it was. Across the road, directly in front of us, the beautiful vanilla ice-cream cone rotated high atop The Dairy Freeze.

Daddy rolled down his coal-grime-covered window to check for oncoming traffic. I held my breath while he changed gears. His foot tapped the gas pedal. When the traffic cleared, he would pull out and turn right.

I put the gas stick on his lap, climbed out of my seat and scrunched between his seat and the plywood. With my arm stuck out the window and pointed across the road, I whispered in his ear, "Turn this way."

I braced myself, prepared for him to turn right like he always did. If he did, I would crawl back into my seat. I would sit perfectly still and stare straight ahead until we arrived home. When would it be my turn? To get anything, you had to take turns. I had figured that out. I just didn't know when my turn would come.

Daddy stared straight ahead. He patted the pedal so the engine wouldn't die. He looked up and down the road once more, and he drove straight across the highway into The Dairy Freeze parking lot.

The huge vanilla ice-cream cone was even prettier up close, but it got kind of blurry when my eyes filled with tears.

Daddy removed a small, worn change purse from his bibbed overalls and looked carefully among the few coins. I turned my face upward to him and smiled as he handed me a nickel. I kicked hard on the rusted door to get it open and hopped down.

Just as I had rehearsed in my mind at least a hundred times, I walked slowly to the small window, my head held high. I placed the nickel on the counter and looked at the young girl in the white hat. "One frozen custard," I said.

The girl's lips parted as she stared at my dirty face and clothes, her gaze shifting to our rusted-to-death Blue Goose. Her eyes found Daddy, who watched me from his open window. Soon another girl stepped up to stare, then another. They stepped away and whispered for a few seconds. I worried they wouldn't let me have the ice cream.

But the first girl turned and fixed my ice-cream cone, wrapped a napkin around it, and bent low, so she could reach it to me. I hoped she wouldn't notice the dirt on my hands.

"Here, honey." She slid the nickel back to me. "There's no charge."

"Thank you!" I said. I carefully balanced my ice-cream cone as I climbed into the truck, and I handed the nickel back to Daddy. I didn't even think of keeping it.

When we got home, Daddy and I were too tired to unload the coal, and Mommy and Margaret were asleep.

"We'll sell it first thing tomorrow," Daddy said.

I washed up for bed, and even though I was thirsty, I didn't want to rinse away the taste of that vanilla ice-cream cone. I mimicked Daddy's words, telling myself, "I'll do it first thing tomorrow."

Rosa Casey Evans, Kathy's mother, and John West Evans, Kathy's father

The Blue Goose

I dumped the dirty sink water over the porch banister and came back into the kitchen. Our house had no plumbing. Every day we hauled buckets of water and heated it on the stove for washing dishes and bathing. Afterward, we placed a bucket underneath the sink to catch dirty water, and when it was full, we dumped it in the yard. We used a small outhouse across the creek.

Mommy was standing in front of the open cabinet door and looking at the near empty shelf. It was Daddy who spoke.

"See if the shovel's in the truck, Kathy," he said. He grabbed his tool box. "I'll be ready to go in a minute." I nodded and put on my shoes sitting near the door. I never had to worry about losing anything in our little house because there was nowhere for anything to hide.

In addition to the stove and table, we had a refrigerator, a kitchen cabinet with a rooster painted on the door, and a small sink propped up on four posts. A calendar with a picture of Jesus holding a lamb hung on the wall beside the cabinet. Light from a window over the sink lit up the two little dark rooms, but there were no curtains. Mommy covered the window at night with a piece of cardboard. Electric cords about three feet long hung from the center of the ceilings with lightbulbs attached at the ends. We tugged on short strings hanging from the sockets to turn on the bulbs.

Mommy was quiet as she pulled a package of noodles and a can of tomato soup from the cabinet. She turned to Daddy. "We can have spaghetti today, but I need flour to make biscuits."

"I'll get flour, Rosie," he nodded as he spoke.

On our way out, Daddy stopped at the side of the house and surveyed our coal pile. His eyes fell on the small stack of overnighters—the largest lumps. No matter what season, our coal pile stood as high as our house. Summer was no exception.

"Somethin' wrong, Daddy?" I asked.

"Naw. We have enough."

I remembered what happened before with the coal pile. One cold night, after we had gone to bed, we heard the thump of coal being dropped into buckets. Someone was stealing our coal. Daddy didn't get up to see who was taking it. He never did. He whispered from across the bedroom, "Everyone lay real quiet."

The next morning, I asked him what we were going to do about people taking our coal. He smiled. "There's nothing wrong with wanting to keep warm," he said. "Some folks just got busy and forgot to work on their coal supply." He took a sip from his coffee cup. "Besides, we have plenty, and there's nothing wrong with sharing."

Now I watched as Daddy tossed a couple pieces of scrap iron onto the junk pile. I walked to The Blue Goose, traced a finger along the faded fender, and opened the door. Rust coated the truck from bumper to bumper, although the word *Sunbeam* was still visible through the faded blue paint. The Blue Goose wasn't much to look at, but he was our gift from heaven.

"Did you find the shovel?" Daddy called.

The truck's front door creaked as I pulled it open. My eyes searched the coal lumps in the back end until I spotted the shovel's handle lying on top of the load. "It's in here!" I yelled.

I walked around the truck and tapped on a tire with my foot. The Blue Goose sat patiently and quietly in the cool morning air, as if it were asleep. Once moving, it rolled gently along flat land, but often struggled on the mountains. By the time it was halfway up a hill, it choked and smoked and made a terrible noise under the hood. It had a hood ornament, a large bird with wings extended. I could never decide if that bird really was a goose.

"Throw these in the truck." Daddy handed me two five-gallon buckets. "After we sell the coal, we'll wash The Goose."

Mommy sat down on the porch with Margaret Ann. "Looks like it's going to be a pretty day," she said, looking at the sky. "No clouds anywhere."

She wore one of her few day dresses, a flowered dress that zipped up the front. Her pink blouse and matching full skirt that she called her square dancing outfit hung on a clothes rod in the corner of the bedroom. Often she'd take it down and look at it then hang it back on the rod. I never saw her put it on, and I never saw her square dance. But she clapped and danced around the kitchen on Saturday nights while listening to the Grand Ole Opry.

The image of Mommy dancing suddenly evaporated as Daddy hollered, "Let's go."

We climbed in. I held the door shut with one hand, reached outside, and grabbed the large L-shaped angle iron. It squeaked as I pulled it across the door, locking me inside. Daddy did the same on his side. This was Daddy's idea of keeping us in The Blue Goose because the doors didn't shut all the way, so we held them in place with pieces of iron he'd welded on the outside.

Next came the window cranking. Rolling took a lot of time, because there were no knobs on the handles. You cranked only one-half turn, repositioned your hand, cranked another half-turn, and you cranked again. The windows stopped themselves about two inches from the top of the door, never closing all the way.

Daddy pumped hard on the gas pedal and turned the key. Luckily, today The Goose started the first time. "He's burning oil real bad," Daddy said, revving up the engine. Blue smoke billowed past our house and floated down the holler. "We'll have to check it when we get back."

We pulled out slowly and gently. I held my sticks, waiting for Daddy's instructions. "Press hard on the gas. Don't let up until I tell you." We wobbled on the ruts and soon reached the hardtop. We turned right toward the coal camps. An early-morning sun peeked through the mountaintops of Paint Creek, casting shadows on the road. I sat on the edge of my seat, rested my chin and arms on the dashboard, and stared at the shadows before we ran over them. I looked for animals and scary faces. Sometimes Daddy played, too.

"It wasn't good letting that coal sit on those tires all night," Daddy said. "We'll be lucky if we don't have a blowout."

We came to the first coal camp, but Daddy didn't stop. Last week, only one household needed coal, and several told us to check back in two to three weeks. We drove on to the second coal camp. I didn't mind the extra ride, because I knew we'd pass by my favorite tree. Daddy always slowed down to let me get an extra good look.

Standing on the far side of a narrow bridge, the tree faced the road. Someone had carved a statue of Jesus, standing with his arms outstretched, into the tree. We called it The Jesus Tree. It looked like a picture from a Sunday school lesson. As we drove across the bridge, Jesus looked straight at us. Across the creek, in the same yard, someone had painted on a rock a picture of a woman lying on her side. Her long hair fanned around her. She was beautiful.

There had been a few wrecks on that bridge. When you came up on that tree at night, Jesus looked like he was floating in midair, coming right toward you. People who weren't from around here got so busy looking at Jesus they sometimes ran into the bridge, missed the curve, or drove straight into the creek.

After we passed The Jesus Tree, we arrived at the second one. This coal camp housed the black families, whose men worked in the mines. Daddy pulled off the road. "All right," he began. "I'll drive slowly through the camp and wait at the end of the alley. You knock on each door and ask if anyone wants to buy a load of coal. You hear?"

"Yes, Daddy."

"If anybody says they don't need any, you thank them anyway, and go on to the next house. When you make a sale, step out into the alley and motion for me. Understand?"

I nodded. I knew exactly what to do. I knocked on the door and waited for someone to answer. If it were a child, I was to ask to speak to his parents. I was only to talk with adults. I was to ask them if they wanted to buy a load of house coal. Under no circumstances was I to enter any house.

I knocked on several doors. Finally, I got a sale from a woman halfway down the row. I stepped into the alley and motioned for Daddy to come. He slowly drove The Goose up to the house and backed up to their coal bin. Daddy shoveled coal out of the back end while I crouched inside the truck atop the coal pile and pushed the coal toward the back with my legs. Soon we were on the road again. The Blue Goose didn't squat so bad now, so we didn't have to worry about exploding tires.

Coal dust from piles of coal carried in the back of the truck blew toward the front and encircled our heads. It stung our faces and covered our laps. After a few miles, we turned off the road and drove toward the creek.

"She's a little higher than normal," Daddy said, glancing at the water. "Hop out and watch me back up." I got out of the truck and waited while Daddy pulled up to the side of the hill.

"Don't let me get too close," he said, backing the truck in my direction. "We don't want to float away."

"Come on back," I called, waving my hand. I kept a close eye on the back wheels and the swift-moving current. "Stop! That's far enough." The Goose's wheels almost touched the water.

Daddy opened the back doors and pulled out the buckets. We scooped water from the creek and threw it into the back of the truck. Black coal dirt and crumbled pieces of coal ran out of the empty truck and splashed into the water, turning it black. I climbed inside the truck bed, and Daddy handed me several buckets of water to pour on the inside walls. I rinsed them well and threw water under the two front seats. I was glad we got to wash the truck. There would be no more coal dust and bits flying all over us—that is—until we got another load of coal.

Daddy pointed to the ridge line on the other side of the creek. "Those look like storm clouds," he said. "Might get some rain." We stood outside for several minutes while the grayish water drained and dripped from the truck—the same color as the few large clouds that drifted over the mountain.

After The Goose dried a bit, Daddy loaded the buckets into the back, and we climbed in and closed the doors. The old wooden floor planks still looked black. They never came clean, not even after a good rinsing.

In no time, we were back on the dirt road, headed for the hardtop. At the intersection, he paused and looked both ways twice. I pressed the pedal with the gas stick, and we pulled onto the paved road.

We arrived home later with the flour and soon the oven was hot and ready to bake biscuits. While the biscuits baked, Mommy cooked the noodles and dumped in the can of tomato soup. Those biscuits were wonderful. And for a while, we would have plenty to eat. Thanks to the coal sales, our cabinet had potatoes, beans, canned milk, lard, coffee, and cornmeal. A full belly once more.

Later that evening, I sat on the porch and listened to Mommy and Daddy play the guitar. We took turns holding Margaret Ann. Daddy went first with "Candy Kisses" and "Groundhog." I loved singing with him, especially funny songs like "Please Pass the Biscuits." Daddy handed the guitar to Mommy, and after she tuned it, she sang two of her favorites, "Hey Good Lookin" and "I Walk the Line." Daddy and I clapped and Mommy smiled. She adjusted the bobby pins in her hair, strummed a few chords and began one of my favorites, "Catch a Falling Star." She let me sing with her on that one.

A warm breeze drifted down the holler and within a few minutes, a cooler breeze followed by a warmer one. Lightning flashed on the far ridge. Mommy stopped playing and fidgeted around. Another flash lit up the woods near the house. She held the guitar upright in her lap and scooted to the edge of the chair. She stared at the sky. "I'm going in," she said. She set the guitar inside the door and came back for Margaret, who was still clapping her little hands.

Daddy calmly puffed on his cigarette. "It'll be okay. Just a summer storm," he said.

A bright bolt flashed the yard and lit up The Blue Goose parked beside the house. "The Goose needs more washing," Daddy said. "Can barely see out the windows."

Soon thunder crashed overhead and heavy rain slammed onto the porch. Daddy and I followed Mommy inside. A little while later the thunder and lightning stopped, but the rain beat hard on the roof. Mommy was scared of storms and didn't get around water when it was lightning. Once the threat of lightning was gone, she allowed me to wash Big Ben in her aluminum dishpan. Although I got him squeaky clean, underneath all that dirt, he was scarred and worn. He needed a paint job, just like The Goose.

The Blue Goose
Noah sitting on the hood, Kathy standing with hands clasped

Treasures Along the Mile

The June rain lasted several days. It flooded yards, fields, and gardens.

"Hurry up and get dressed," Daddy said, standing over the bed. "The creek's gone down, and it's a toyland down there."

I sat up and rubbed my sleepy eyes. "What toys?"

"Sssh!" He put his finger to his mouth. "Margaret Ann's asleep."

I threw back the blanket, dangled my feet over the bed and hopped down.

"We have to go now, or someone else will get there first. The sun's out, and I've already been scouting. There's a mile or more of treasures waiting for us."

I went to the porch. A few piles of dirty clothes lay scattered near the washer. Mommy stuffed a load into the Maytag and turned the lever. Quickly, the motor kicked in and began churning the clothes. "Be careful down there," she said, pointing toward the creek. "You can't swim, and if you fall in, your Daddy couldn't save you."

"I'll be careful," I said.

I climbed on the bannister and looked out over the top of the trees to the creek below. Paper and plastic hung on trees and bushes near the creek. Stray logs and garbage lay in the road. Paint Creek was back in her bed, but she'd left a long pile of sand strewn up and down the road. Even now, back within her banks, she still roared.

"Come on," he said, grabbing his walking stick and empty seed bag.

I followed him down the holler, crossing a field to the road. As we got closer, the sound of rushing water from the rain-swollen creek grew louder.

"Be careful crossing the road. It may be washed out in places, so let me go first."

He punched the sand with his stick several times before taking a step and motioned me to follow. I watched his every move and stepped in his tracks.

At the creek bank, he pointed his walking stick. "See. I told you."

I was surprised. It was nothing like the county dump with its broken furniture, mattress springs, wire tubing, rope, pop bottles, and old radios. There, stuck in the sand, was a set of wooden steps, part of a porch, and several logs wedged behind a huge rock. And up ahead I saw the toyland. I might get lucky and find another treasure like Big Ben!

"Wow!" I jumped up and down. "I might find me something real good!" I had been treasure hunting before, but not here—not like this.

Beautiful bright reds and yellows stuck out of the sand as if to say, "I'm here, Kathy! Come and get me!" Shiny chrome handlebars peeped around rocks wedged between piles of wood. I couldn't wait to get to the free toys.

"I want that red thing down there." I didn't know what it was, but the color was so bright, it had to be good.

"Now, hold on," Daddy said. "Stay next to me and watch where you put your foot. The current's moving fast, and I don't want us to fall in. Stay on the bank."

Soft, squishy sandbars lined the banks. They smelled like stagnant mud puddles. Once in a while, a stinky breeze blew our way. I pinched my nostrils closed.

Daddy led me to the red thing. I picked it up and turned it over. We couldn't figure out what it was, so we left it and walked on. He poked holes in the sand and dug out anything partially buried.

He found a nice pot lid, round with a black knob, and he put it into the bag. "We can use this." A small, gold jewelry box, about the size of a napkin, went into the bag. Next, he held up a large metal bucket by its handle. "This will be good to carry coal in."

Daddy took his time picking up a few things here and there, while I wandered ahead to a large sand pile near the bank. I jabbed my stick into the sand and turned over something metal.

"What're you lookin' at?" Daddy yelled.

"Something red. It has handlebars. A window frame's on top of it." I tugged hard.

"Be careful. There's broken glass around there."

Daddy walked over and looked at the piece of metal. He bent low, grabbed it with his good hand and yanked. Out came a red scooter.

I sucked in a breath. "Can I ride it? Can I ride it?" I jumped up and down. "It's the best toy ever!"

Daddy examined the scooter and nodded. "After it's fixed. It's missing a wheel."

I suppose Daddy picked up another find or two, but if he did, I don't remember. I held tight to one handlebar, Daddy held the other, and together we dragged home the best toy I'd ever owned, my new scooter. Big Ben was very special, but nothing compared to the scooter!

First Ride

It was the first of July when Daddy finally got around to working on the scooter. I couldn't wait to ride.

I finished the last bite of oatmeal and ran to the front porch. He was in the yard working near the back wheel. "Daddy," I said, "Mommy said to tell you that breakfast is ready."

He nodded. "That's all I can do for now." He put down his tools. He'd searched until he found a wheel in the junk pile that fit the scooter.

"Can I ride it now?" I asked.

"No, there's nothing to hold the wheel in place. It needs a cotter key. Leave it alone until I can find one."

I bounced heel to toe. "But the wheel's on, and it turns."

"A nail's holding the axle. It'll come out as soon as you get on. I'll get a cotter key after I eat."

I slid my hand over the handlebars. One rubber grip was missing, but I didn't care. The scooter was scratched and rusted, but it was my dream toy.

"Now don't go riding it." Daddy wagged a finger in my direction. "It's not ready."

Mommy called him again to breakfast. I pulled my tea set from a box on the porch, along with a couple of tin cans, so I could play house in the yard. My makeshift kitchen table was an old board spread across two large lumps of coal Daddy had placed in front of the porch. I spent hours pretending to cook and serve tea to my red-haired doll with one blinking eye. The stream that ran near the front porch made it easy to get water for my mud pies.

I picked up a tin can and started toward the creek to get some water, but my feet walked me right over to the scooter instead.

I put down the can and stroked the handlebars. Next, I lifted the scooter by the handlebars and rolled it a few feet. It rolled just fine. I gripped the handlebars, rested one foot on the platform and pushed with the other foot. I even made circles. I strolled up and down the flat dirt yard, smiling and giggling.

I rolled my scooter to the edge of the yard. Riding a scooter would be easy. I couldn't wait!

But the yard was too small. I really wanted a good ride. I rolled the scooter to the holler road. The road was flat, but a recent washout had left small rocks behind. I wasn't worried, though. I'd rolled the scooter through our lumpy old yard, so the rocks on the road's smooth surface should be easy. I pushed the scooter up the hill to an old garage and turned it around.

This will be a good ride!

At the top of the hill, I positioned the scooter in the middle of the road and looked around. Down below, our two-room house hugged the mountainside. Gray smoke curled out of the stovepipe and lazily drifted down the holler. The screen door opened, and Mommy threw a pan of dishwater over the banister. I held my breath, but she didn't notice me, and she turned and went back inside.

In front of me, ruts shaped by spring rains and hardened by the sun furrowed the steep dirt road. High weeds and thick bushes framed both sides, making a trip down the hill scary. I wanted to ride so bad. Surely I would be okay. I rolled the scooter back and forth, remembering Daddy's words about the wheel. But the wheels still turned easily. *It'll be okay. I pushed it all the way up here, and the wheel didn't fall off. Now step on and push off. It'll be a great ride!*

I gripped the handlebars and took one last look down the rutty road. I placed the scooter's wheels in the smoothest part of the road between the ruts, took a deep breath, and pushed off. The scooter went faster and faster. Way too fast. I held on as tight as I could, but I was in trouble. The scooter dipped into a rut, came out, threw me into another rut, and another. Suddenly the back wheel flew off, and I flew forward. The scooter and I both tumbled down the hill.

I landed in the creek. "Help!" I screamed. I cried and splashed as I pushed away potato peelings, tin cans, and other garbage that had washed into the swollen creek. The high water moved fast. As hard as I tried to get out, it kept taking me farther and farther away, pushing me toward the culvert. I kicked and grabbed at everything that floated by, but the creek was too powerful for my small body. At the last minute, I grabbed for the ridged edge of the culvert, and I caught it. I clung hard to the sharp edge, cutting the end of my finger.

Mommy flew out of the house. She ran toward me faster than I'd ever seen her move, and without even pausing, she waded into the creek, its dirty water parting around her. She pulled me out of the culvert and carried me to the porch. Daddy hobbled outside, handed a screaming Margaret Ann to Mommy and walked along the bank and peered into the creek. I sniffled as Mommy took me inside and helped me change clothes.

A few minutes later, we came outside and sat on the porch. Mommy dabbed my many cuts and scrapes with Mercurochrome, and I winced and whimpered at the stinging it caused. She bandaged the cut on my finger, and when I looked up, Daddy held the runaway wheel in his hand. He stared at the scooter that lay on the bank, turned his head, and scowled at me. Limping to the back of the truck, he opened the rear doors and flung the wheel inside. He picked up the scooter, tossed it inside, and slammed the doors shut.

I never saw my scooter again. That night in bed I cried for my scooter, my dream toy. If only I had listened to Daddy, I would still have it. Before I fell asleep, I reached down at the foot of the bed and felt for Big Ben. He was still there.

Duz or Breeze?

It was the end of July. The first day of August, the welfare check would arrive, and we'd make a trip to the A & P Supermarket. Margaret Ann slept, and I lay in bed and watched my parents from the open doorway. I listened to them while they sat at the porcelain table and worked on the grocery list: flour, cornmeal, sugar, potatoes, beans, dry milk. Detergent came last.

"What will it be?" Daddy asked. "A box of Duz or a box of Breeze?"

"I don't know," Mommy said, tilting her head to one side. The question required thought. After all, a free towel was included in every box of Breeze. But a free cup or saucer was included in boxes of Duz. You never knew which one you would get. We had only two cups, so a cup was more valuable to Mommy. Most of the time, the box contained only another flat saucer.

"Well, which one did we buy last month?" Daddy asked.

"I think we got Breeze. No. No, it was Duz. I remember burning the box the other day."

Daddy rubbed his chin. "What do we need most, towels or dishes?"

Mommy's shoulder lifted and dropped. "Let's get Breeze. We can always use another towel." Depending on the size of the box, Breeze gave you a bath towel, hand towel, or washcloth. Mommy once sewed six bath towels together to make a spread for the bed, and she used a couple of washcloths as doilies. We wouldn't afford the beautiful counterpins sold at the roadside gift shops on Route 60. These white bedspreads with pink and green flowers hung on lines in front of the store; some were decorated with red and blue peacocks. Mommy stared at them when we passed by, but we never stopped.

She counted the small stack of towels folded on the corner of the kitchen cabinet. I loved the colorful rooster painted on the flour-bin side because to me, it looked real, and was the prettiest thing in the kitchen. In addition to the towels, the cabinet held a few dishes, pots and pans, and groceries.

Daddy tapped the table. "But the other day you said you wanted a cup. That means we need to get a box of Duz."

"Well, okay." Mommy stood and rinsed out the coffeepot. "I'm not sure which one we need."

"That settles it," he said. "Tomorrow we'll get a box of Breeze. Write *Breeze* on the store list."

Mommy returned to the table, wrote on the store list, folded it, and slipped it into her purse. Daddy stood, picked up the coal bucket, and headed out to refill it.

Mommy pulled out the cigarette roller. Carefully, she opened a small blue pouch and poured a small amount of tobacco into the long, narrow opening on one side of the roller and patted the tobacco with her finger. She licked a small piece of paper the length of a cigarette and placed it above the tobacco. Next, she grabbed the lever and rolled it up, down, and over the other side. Out rolled a cigarette. She made one more and left them lying on the table.

While Daddy gathered coal, Mommy pulled her chair near the warm kitchen stove and pin curled her hair. She dampened each strand of hair with water, wrapped it around her finger and pinned it to her head with black bobby pins. When she removed the pins from her thick, black hair, it lay in beautiful curls all over her head. She barely ran the comb through it to fix it. My hair was straight with bangs. I wished I had curly hair like Mommy's.

Daddy came back a few minutes later. He tossed a couple lumps of coal into the kitchen stove and pulled up a chair to join Mommy.

I watched out the bedroom doorway as my folks smoked their bedtime Buglers. Soon, the ends of the cigarettes burned golden orange. When the smoke drifted into the bedroom, I slipped my head under the covers because I did not like the smell. Their voices lowered, and, after a few minutes, I barely heard them at all. Finally, I slept.

The A & P Supermarket, as usual, was crowded on check day. Most shoppers used two shopping carts, including my parents. Large bags of flour, cornmeal, and potatoes went into the bottom of the carts. Cartons of eggs were stacked on top of lard buckets, and a month's supply of bread filled the child seats.

Mommy and Daddy pushed their carts through the aisles and made their selections. After a while, they paused to check the grocery list.

"Did you get pinto beans?" Daddy asked.

"Yes, four bags," Mommy said. "Did you get catsup and mustard?"

"Yes, and mayonnaise. Did you get the jelly and detergent?"

Mommy's finger traced down the list. "That's it," she said. "I knew I forgot something. Detergent. I didn't get any detergent."

Mommy and Daddy pushed their stuffed carts to the detergent aisle and stared at the boxes of soap. I crept along behind them. Red, orange, blue, and green writing shouted from the fronts of the boxes. They fixed their eyes on a bright red box of Breeze. Mommy picked up a large one that displayed a pink-and-orange-striped bath towel. She set it back on the shelf.

In an instant, she pushed the cart a few feet further. Her brown eyes widened. She gaped at the shiny teacups and saucers pictured on a box of Duz. Her hand hovered in the air beside the box for a moment before she finally touched it. Daddy stood quietly as she placed the large box of Duz on the top of the cart. Suddenly, Mommy turned the cart around and headed for the checkout, her smile leading the way. I couldn't wait to see what was inside.

Later that day, she cut off the top of the box, dug her hand inside, and felt around. Within a few seconds, she pulled out a bright shiny cup.

She smiled. "This makes three!" I clapped. Now I had one.

She was so happy to get another cup that she removed everything from the cabinet and wiped it down inside and out. Next, she rearranged the few plates and saucers and placed the three cups in a row on the front shelf. She must have overdone the cleaning because that was the last time she was able to do anything for the entire month of August; at least it seemed that was the reason.

Kathy's Dad and his Aunt Viola
She's removing a splinter from his hand

First Year in School

August was not a happy month. Mommy threw up every morning and had to lie down afterward. Although she felt a little better in the afternoon, Daddy cooked and I watched Margaret Ann. Mommy never picked up the guitar or sang any songs. One day Mrs. Johnson, a widow who lived below us, stopped by. She went into the bedroom and talked with Mommy and Daddy. I never heard what they said, but she smiled at me when she left.

Near the end of August, Mommy cooked and did laundry again. She washed my clothes first and hung them on the lines to dry. "School starts next week," she said.

Daddy drove me to school on the first day, and on the way there, he showed me a path I'd walk to get to the main road from then on. He told me to wait near the road for older kids and cross the road with them. The school was a short walk on the other side of the creek. I nodded and Daddy pulled up to the school and shut off the motor.

He pointed to the wooden building. "There's only two rooms. The one on this end is where you'll go."

A row of windows lined the front side of the building, and a small outhouse stood near the hill. Taller students entered a door on the far end. A woman stood at the top of the steps and rang a handbell.

"That bell means class is starting," Daddy said. "Time to go." He patted me on the head. Mommy and Daddy never hugged us or each other, but a pat on the head was good.

I pushed the door open, hopped out and shut it behind me, and pulled the iron bar back in place. Daddy started the motor and drove away. I looked around, but I didn't recognize any of the faces. There were two houses in our holler, but the kids who lived in them were older than me, and I didn't know them. I hoped to meet someone that I could play with and talk to at recess.

I followed the other kids inside and stood in the back with them. Now the woman who rang the bell stood in front of the room—straight and tall as a statue. She never smiled. Six rows of wooden desks fastened to the floor faced her, their seats folded up.

"I am Mrs. Ballard," she said. She pointed to a row on the right. "First grade sits here." A few students scrambled to the desks in front of me, leaving one in the back. I sat there. She continued pointing. "Row two is for second grade, row three for third grade." She stopped at the last row when she announced sixth grade.

A teacher's desk sat up front in the corner, ABC's and numbers ran above the blackboard, and stacks of papers covered a long table. In the back of the room, a small table sat behind a half-opened curtain. The door to the other classroom opened and two boys entered. They carried a large white crock. I'd seen one like this before with pickles inside. "Where do you want this?" one of them asked.

"Back table," she said and led the way.

A student placed a sheet of paper on every desk. Mrs. Ballard pushed the curtain all the way back, revealing the crock sitting on the table. "This is your drinking water. You will get a drink twice a day—morning and afternoon."

She held out a sheet of white paper. "Watch carefully." She folded the paper so fast and in so many directions that I couldn't keep up. I was backwards and couldn't use my desk to fold the paper. The older student's cups looked great, but mine didn't. Now I wouldn't get my drink of water. I did not like her, and I did not like school.

"Throw your empty cups in this bucket when you are finished at the end of the day. No paper on the floor. The lunch bell will ring at

12 o'clock. Those who brought lunch will eat at their desks or outside. Walkers, you may walk home but return by 1:00. I expect everyone to be seated when the bell rings at 1:00." She scared me. I would rather be at the dump with Daddy or picking berries. Anywhere but here. I'm not sure what lesson she taught. I only remember her giving out papers to each row and hearing pencils scribbling on the desktops.

Later that morning, a girl in front of me raised her hand. The teacher looked up and ignored her. She raised her hand again. "May I go to the toilet?" she asked.

Mrs. Ballard looked at her watch. "No. It's not time. Lunch is in fifteen minutes. You can wait."

The girl squirmed in her seat. She put her head down on the desk, crossed her legs and squirmed some more. The older students kept working and paid no attention. A few seconds later, water splattered the floor, and I smelled something. I looked down in time to see pee running under my desk. I lifted my feet off the floor.

Kids looked around and held their noses. The girl in front of me kept her head down on the desk. The back of her dress and seat were wet. Mrs. Ballard grabbed a wooden paddle from the top of her desk and walked down the row. She yanked her out of her seat, took her to the back, and closed the curtain. I heard three paddle whacks. Mrs. Ballard opened the curtain, walked the girl to her seat, and said, "I told you to hold it." She put her head down and cried. I felt sorry for her, but I felt sorry for me too because I had nowhere to put my feet. Mrs. Ballard rang the lunch bell, and as soon as she dismissed our row, I ran out.

I followed some kids across the road and shot up the path Daddy showed me. Mommy had a hot bowl of beans waiting for me, and Daddy wasn't home. I told her about the girl peeing in her seat. "Make sure you go to the toilet before school starts," she said. "And do what the teacher says." I never said anything else.

I knew right there that I had to be good. I remembered the terrible switching Mommy gave me a few months ago because I never answered her when she called me in from playing. Those welts lasted for days.

And Daddy spanked me really hard because a neighbor told him I hit her little boy with a rock. Daddy never said a word, but turned me over his lap and spanked me. I cried all evening. Later that night, the woman apologized and said her son had fibbed. Daddy lifted me on his lap and told me he was sorry, but I couldn't sit well for a week. Those two whippings taught me to do what I was told.

As Daddy had instructed, I walked the path to the road and waited for the other kids. I crossed the road when they did, and was in my seat before the bell rang.

Several weeks passed, and I noticed Mommy's belly poked out a little, making her dresses tight. Finally, she told me we were having a new baby in the spring. I would be six and a half, and Margaret Ann would be almost two when it arrived. I was happy for two reasons: I was getting a new baby brother or sister to play with, and I was learning how to make my own paper cup.

Soon winter snow and sickness set in. I missed school because of deep snows, or I was sick with sore throats, colds, or the flu. Often, The Goose couldn't make it out of the holler because of bald tires. Whenever Daddy could make it out, he searched the dump and creek bank looking for things he could sell for scrap. Sometimes he sold a small load of coal and bought groceries. Thank goodness *we* didn't need any coal. Daddy worked in the summer to gather enough for us.

The weather wasn't the only thing that prevented me from going to school. I took care of Mommy or Margaret Ann when they were sick. One day while Mommy and Margaret Ann were asleep, Daddy cooked a pot of beans. He was busy mixing cornbread batter and asked me to put a teaspoon of salt in the beans. I did.

An hour later, he tasted them. "How much salt did you put in here?" he asked.

I showed him the spoon. "This one. Heaping full."

He frowned and pointed his finger at me. "That's not a teaspoon. That's a tablespoon! They're too salty and can't be eaten like this. Get me four potatoes."

He cut the potatoes in half and dumped them into the pot. "The potatoes will draw the salt from the beans." I felt bad that I used the wrong spoon, but also because we had to use potatoes that we could have saved for another meal. I promised myself that I would pay attention next time.

When Mommy and Margaret Ann got better, I went back to school, but by that time I was far behind and had trouble keeping up. I had missed several alphabet and math lessons. One day Mrs. Ballard used a flannel board to teach math. She stood in front of our row and placed ducks on the flannel board. She added and removed them and asked students questions. I watched her but didn't understand what she was doing. The room felt hot, and I didn't feel so well.

She asked a question and called on me. I looked at the board and at the ducks, but nothing came to me. She grabbed her paddle, lifted me out of my seat, and gave me two paddle whacks. My rear-end stung. "Stop daydreaming!" she said. I didn't like Mrs. Ballard, and I still didn't like school.

That evening I developed a fever, and Mommy put me in bed. She asked Mrs. Johnson to check on me. She always asked her for advice when we were sick. She felt my forehead, looked in my throat, and raised my shirt. "See that rash?" she said. Mommy leaned in to take a better look. Mrs. Johnson pointed to my belly. "It's measles." Now, Daddy took care of everybody.

I got over the measles and went to school again, but a few weeks later, I came home with swollen cheeks. Mrs. Johnson came again. I had mumps. I slept most of the time and don't remember too much of what went on around the house, except that Daddy busied himself in the kitchen when I was awake. I went back to school after a couple of weeks and knew I'd be behind again.

December came and so did Christmas. Mrs. Ballard let us cut out red and green paper bells and tape them on the windows. I was proud of my little red bell stuck up there with the other kids. There were no decorations at home. The only thing I got for Christmas was chicken pox. Mrs. Johnson told Mommy positively to not go near me. Chicken pox could harm the baby. Daddy took care of me.

January 1959 came, but I wasn't ready to go back to school. Mommy and Daddy thought it was good for me to have had measles, mumps, and chicken pox in my first year of school. They said I wouldn't have to be bothered with them anymore, and I wouldn't have to miss so much school next year. Mommy said I'd be ready to go back in another week. Her swollen belly made it difficult to walk and care for Margaret Ann. She wasn't able to sit and play the guitar or sing anymore. Daddy kept a roaring fire in the potbelly stove in the bedroom and kept extra wood and coal stacked in the house.

In February, I settled back in school. Daddy stayed home most of the time and helped Mommy unless he was picking up coal to sell. I listened to Mrs. Ballard as best I could and was beginning to like school a little better. Then something happened.

During our morning water break, students got in line to get their dipper of water. The first two students complained about the look and taste of the water. They gagged and made faces. They showed their paper cups with the milky color to Mrs. Ballard. She took off the lid to the crock, looked inside, and removed a white bar of soap. The same soap we washed our hands with before lunch and after using the toilet.

She held the bar in front of her. "Who did this?" she asked. "How did this soap get in here?"

She stared at everyone eyeball to eyeball. The girl in front of me who had peed her pants did not look at Mrs. Ballard. Instead, she looked down at her desk. Mrs. Ballard noticed. "Hannah, did you do this?"

Hannah lowered her head and cried. "Yes," she said.

Mrs. Ballard grabbed the paddle and gave her three whacks. "There'll be no water today. The crock has to be taken home and washed."

Why would Hannah put the soap in the crock? I guessed it was to get even with Mrs. Ballard for paddling her on the first day of school. But Hannah didn't have to punish everybody. We all drank from that crock.

At the end of March, I came home from school and found Mommy in bed holding my new baby brother, Noah. He was tiny and looked like Margaret and me—brown hair and eyes. Again, I stayed home to help Daddy care for everyone. Of course, I got behind in school. But as soon as I could, I went back. I had worked hard to learn the alphabet, and after a while, I could read. I was so happy the day I ran home and read the words carved on Big Ben's statue: *At the Wheel for a New Deal*. I even read the word *Roosevelt* written above those words. I was beginning to like school after all.

On the last day of school in May, Mrs. Ballard rang the handbell for the last time. I hurried across the bottom with the other kids, crossed the road, and began the path toward our house. As I started up the hill to our house, a woman came out our door and shouted, "You's cut off! Mr. Evans, you's cut off!" Her words scared me.

"Get outa my yard!" Daddy yelled at her as I came into view.

A heavy-set black woman hurried from the porch. Daddy unbuckled his peg leg belts. He grasped the leg, held it high, and threw it at the woman. The woman screamed and ran to a green car parked beside our coal pile. The peg leg missed the car by only a few inches, landed hard, and skidded several feet across the yard into the road. The woman spun out into the road, left in a cloud of dust, and didn't slow down for the ruts or curves. The car squeaked and groaned as it bounced down the road and out of sight.

Daddy shook his head. "Bring me my leg, Kathy." He held onto the porch banister for balance as I ran across the road, picked up the leg, and carried it up the steps. He strapped the belts around his waist and upper thigh and sat down with a thump.

Mommy appeared at the screen door with two-month-old Noah and two-year-old Margaret Ann. Dark circles under her eyes looked like smudges of coal. She hadn't been well since Noah was born. "Is she gone?" Mommy asked.

"Yeah," Daddy said. "She won't be back."

"Who was she?" I asked.

They were both quiet at first. Mommy jiggled Noah and Daddy looked off toward the other side of the road. Mommy finally explained. "The woman was a Welfare Investigator. She cut us off welfare because she heard we were selling coal." Mommy's eyes were shiny with tears. "People who receive welfare are not allowed to earn money." She jiggled Noah a little more.

Daddy took over. Slowly he said, "You have a little sister that died when she was two months old. We were selling coal to pay for her funeral. We almost had it paid off, too." He continued to look across the road.

When the first of June came, we were nearly out of food. Daddy went to the post office and called for the mail. No check. He went again the next day and the next. The postmaster checked all the other boxes for us, but there was no check. That woman meant what she said.

A couple of weeks later, Daddy found out that he could re-apply for welfare in another county if he was a resident. He sold scrap iron to buy gas for The Goose, and the next day he left Kanawha County to go house hunting.

Kathy with Santa and Noah

Rosie's calendars with pictures of Jesus

Moving Day

Daddy searched and searched until he found a rental house in Logan County. He proudly told Mommy the news. "It rents for $20.00 a month plus repairs."

"We can't afford that," Mommy said. "This place is free because we built it ourselves, and we still have a hard time."

"We'll manage somehow," Daddy said. I held Noah while Daddy and Mommy packed the Maytag, refrigerator, radio, sewing machine, sink, and wash tubs. He took them to the new house and didn't get home until after dark. I was asleep when he got home.

That morning, there was no fire in the stove, nor any breakfast cooked. "Don't have time to build a fire," Mommy said. "We need to get this last load to Logan before dark." Daddy pulled up and got out of The Goose, carrying a small bag. It had a package of bologna, a loaf of bread, and one bunch of bananas. "This will have to do until we get to Logan," he said. I didn't know where he got the money, and I wasn't about to ask. I was hungry. I reached for a banana and peeled it slowly.

I didn't understand why we had to move. "Maybe if you tell them why we sell coal, they'll change their mind."

"This is the middle of July," Mommy said. "They've had plenty of time to change their minds. We were cut off in May."

She slid slices of bologna in between pieces of bread, making three sandwiches, and put the leftovers in the box she was packing. "You're not supposed to make any money when you're on welfare. They cut your check and your father can't work." I wasn't sure I understood her.

"Check on your sister," Mommy said. She worked quickly and didn't look up. Noah would soon be awake.

I checked the front porch. "Margaret's okay. Playing on the porch with plastic cups you gave her."

I watched Mommy pack some more and at last I asked, "How'd they find out?"

"People report you. They'll tell if you have a TV or own a vehicle."

We didn't have a TV. I pointed to the truck parked in the front yard. "What about The Goose? She belongs to us."

"No, she doesn't," Daddy said. "That truck belongs to my uncle who lives in Logan County." I didn't understand any of this except that we worked hard to get food.

Daddy put our two beds, a kitchen table, and three wooden chairs into the back of the truck. Mommy's kitchen cabinet with the rooster decal on the front went in last; he strapped the mattresses on top and closed the front door. The cast iron cook stove stayed with the house because Daddy said the new house had a gas cook stove. We all climbed in and waited quietly.

"There he is." Daddy pointed to a man walking up the holler.

The man carried a box on his shoulder, so I couldn't see his face. Daddy got out of the truck and stood beside the door. We watched the stranger approach. The man handed Daddy a box, and he put it behind his seat in The Goose. The two of them shook hands and said some howdy-dos. Daddy pointed to his one-story high coal pile beside the house and homemade wooden swing on the front porch. The man nodded at everything Daddy said, and they shook hands again. The man turned around and walked back the way he came. Daddy got in and started the motor.

"Did you get it?" Mommy asked. "Did he pay you?"

"Yes," Daddy said, driving away. "He gave me what I asked for, plus ten dollars to boot."

"Well, at least that's a start. Every little bit helps," she said.

Loaded down, The Blue Goose rocked and bumped along the deeply rutted road. Daddy took it slowly, driving carefully down the hill. Before we rounded the first curve, I opened the lid to the box and peeked inside. I counted thirty cans of evaporated milk. I closed the lid and took one last look at the shack—my home—our coal pile, the little creek I played in, and the outhouse on the side of the hill.

When the trees blinded my view, I turned around and faced the front. I wondered where Daddy was taking us. Where would we go? Where would we live? And, as I often wondered, even before the welfare checks stopped coming, how would we have enough to eat?

Our New House

We were cramped on the long drive to Logan. Table and chair legs poked my back, and my feet jammed against the box of canned milk and Daddy's peg leg. Margaret and I sat behind Mommy and Daddy's seats on a long board propped up with cinderblocks. Not long after we pulled out of Paint Creek, Margaret nodded off, and I eased her across my lap so she could sleep. Noah slept on Mommy's lap, but I kept watching the road, anxious to see where Daddy was taking us. Later, I saw the road sign that pointed to Logan.

"We're almost there," Daddy said. Later, he turned onto Mud Fork Road. The Goose struggled when Daddy changed gears, and Mommy helped him drive when he asked her. I took in all that I saw. A small creek and a railroad track ran alongside the paved road, and mountains hugged either side of us. Rows of houses lined the road. A few were spread a short distance from each other, while others perched together on hillsides. We drove a few more miles, and Daddy slowed down. He looked around. "We're getting close," he said.

We passed a small white church beside the road. It reminded me of the one Mommy took me to on Paint Creek. We didn't stay long. Mommy grabbed me by the hand and hurried out the door. "It's too hot in there," she said. She hesitated and listened to the preaching through the opened windows for a few minutes before she tugged on my hand, and we walked home. I wondered why we didn't stay in the building and fan ourselves with one of those paper fans.

Daddy pointed to a small brown building on the left. "That's our post office," he said. I took a quick peek before he spoke again.

"And there's the name of the place we'll be living in." He pointed to a sign across the road from the flagpole—VERDUNVILLE. "Our house is over there." He pointed to a group of houses behind the sign.

A few feet above the post office sat The Island Creek Coal Company #16 Store. A concrete porch ran the full length of the store, and a phone booth sat in the middle. A few teenagers sat near the steps drinking pop. I couldn't wait to go inside. Although I couldn't see through the large glass storefront windows, I imagined there would be racks of beautiful clothes, shiny new shoes, and boxes of candy bars and gum.

The Blue Goose turned right at the store and crossed the tracks onto a dirt-covered alley. There were five rows of houses, each with four houses side by side with only a few feet in between each one. We turned onto the fourth row and stopped in front of the second house.

"This is it," he said, turning off the motor. "This is the Number Sixteen Camp. It used to be a coal camp. Some coal camps are named, and some are numbered."

We all stayed quiet for a few seconds, taking in our new surroundings. The paint on our yellow rental house had blistered, and ugly gray peeked through. A hint of white remained on the window frames and front door. Daddy pointed to the house beside ours. It was white with a thick grassy yard. "Mr. Williamson lives there. He helped me unload yesterday." Mommy was quiet and stared at our house.

"It's sittin' up kinda high," she said. "Those posts don't look too safe."

"It's fine," Daddy said. "Those concrete posts will hold good. We'll support the weaker ones with cinderblocks, and we'll get some underpinning so the cold air doesn't blow through, come winter."

A wire fence with rough posts lined the front yard, and a cinderblock attached to a chain closed the front gate. A wooden walkway led to the front porch, where every other board was raised, reminding me of the black and white keys on a piano I'd seen in Mrs. Ballard's room. The roof, slightly sunken in the middle, was covered with strips of black tar paper. A cracked brick chimney rose from each side of the house. I couldn't believe we were moving into a house that had so many homes nearby. Surely there would be someone here my age to play with.

"Let's unload," he said. "You can look around later." Daddy unlocked the front door and opened the back doors to the truck. Mommy didn't help unload; instead, she walked into the yard carrying a half-awake Noah. I took Margaret by the hand and followed her.

"Well, at least there's a patch or two of grass," Mommy said, peering around the side of the house. "That makes up for the brown dirt in the front yard."

I followed her to the back of the house, where there were several patches of tall grass. "Well, that's good," Mommy said. She pointed to the two clothesline posts. "At least I can hang out the wash. And there's enough room for the Maytag, too." It sat in a corner of the porch under the kitchen window.

She looked around some more and spotted an old rusted barrel with holes poked in the sides. "That barrel will be good for burning garbage." Nothing else outside. No bushes. No shrubs. No trees. We walked back to the front of the house. A man dressed in dirty gray coveralls and heavy boots helped Daddy untie the mattresses.

Daddy stopped and introduced him. "This is Mr. Williamson."

"Pleased to meet you," Mommy said. "Thanks for helping us." As she spoke, she put her hand to her mouth and partially hid her rotten teeth.

After setting up the beds, Mr. Williamson helped Daddy with the cabinet, then left for work. Daddy explained he worked second shift in the mines up the road. We carried in the last of the boxes. Mommy stopped long enough to fix Noah a bottle with one of the cans of milk we received from the sale of the house. She made the beds, put Noah in the middle of one, and he fell asleep with a pillow scotched by his side.

I toured the house. It had a living room, two bedrooms, a kitchen, a tool room with a hot water heater, and a bathroom with a small round sink, a bathtub with feet, and a commode bottom, without a water tank, but no bathroom door. Each room had a linoleum rug that stopped two feet from each wall.

Mommy stared at the rugs. "Somebody has scrubbed these rugs to death. You can't even make out the pattern anymore." Quietly, she looked around some more. The refrigerator was plugged in, the Philco radio stood alone in the living room, and the Singer sewing machine sat in the front bedroom thanks to Daddy's trip yesterday. I hoped seeing our furniture here would make her like it a little better.

The wallpaper in each room, cracked and stained yellow, needed to be replaced. Each pattern had a flower design except for the kitchen where prints of coffee pots, teapots, and other kitchen gadgets floated along the walls. In some places, the wallpaper strips had peeled away from the ceiling and hung in midair, like limp arms that were tired of holding up the world. Mommy tugged at a few pieces, which loosened other strips.

"It's gonna need some fixin' up," Mommy said. She made her voice sound happier than she clearly felt, "but it's bigger than the two rooms we just moved from."

I nodded and smiled, because I knew that's what she needed me to do.

"When we get on our feet," she said, "we'll get some new wallpaper and paint. Until then I'll put a few calendars on the wall for decoration."

"Yeah, it'll do," Daddy said from the doorway. His leg thumped hollowly against the floor as he crossed the room toward us. "As soon as I can, I'll make a door for the bathroom, but in the meantime, we'll have to put up a sheet. And we'll use a bucket to flush the commode." He waved his half-hand as he spoke. "The bath and kitchen need some plumbing, but I'll get around to that soon as we're on our feet again."

While they talked and planned, I searched for a place for Big Ben to rest. I placed him on the living room hearth and hoped there would be some paint left for him after we fixed up the house. I found Mommy in the bedroom hanging clothes in the tiny closet. The only thing left in the box was Mommy's pink square dancing outfit. She smoothed out the wrinkles in the skirt, held it to her waist, and twirled around. "That's pretty, Mommy. Why don't you wear it?"

She suddenly stopped twirling. "It's for dancing." She hung it on the rod. The closet didn't have a door and the bright pink stood out from the rest of the clothes. "Here." She handed me the empty box. "Take this out to the burn barrel."

I laid the box beside the barrel and looked around our new place. It was different from our holler house, in more ways than one. Most of the nearby houses had aluminum or grainy siding that I'd heard Daddy once call *Insulbrick*. Our neighbors' yards were grassy and neat. A small creek ran behind the store and post office, and a new grade school sat on the hill above our camp houses. I kept looking for someone my age to play with, but all I saw were teenagers. I started to venture out of the yard, but Mommy called us to supper. We ate bologna sandwiches and bananas left over from morning.

That evening, we learned something else about our new home. It had more roaches than we had ever seen. Roaches came scurrying out of the woodwork, from behind the wallpaper, and from beneath the linoleum rugs as we unpacked our boxes. By nightfall, they crawled across the floor and ceiling, and they even ran across the furniture. For a long time, we took turns knocking them down from the walls and ceiling with a broom and stepping on them. We whacked and smacked until we had flattened them all and we went to bed. Mommy slept in one bed with Margaret Ann and Noah, and I slept at the foot of the bed with Daddy, like before, except now I had a window at the foot of the bed.

The best part of having a window was lying in bed watching a silver moon rise. I lay on my side and watched the bright circle move through the tree tops into a black sky. Dark shadows scattered across the yard. It was so beautiful, and I wanted to touch it. Maybe God lived there and was looking down on us right now. It seemed like he might be because we had a new house, and I had the moon in my window.

A light breeze blew through the screen, and I slipped under the covers. As I lay there, I found it hard to believe we now had a house with so many rooms—even an indoor bathroom. No more outhouses! There was plenty of room for us all, now that the roaches were gone.

Kathy's house in Verdunville—front above and back below

Bean Days

Dear God,

Thank you for giving us this house. Please help us get back on Welfare. Mommy is adding water to Noah's milk to make it last, and we're eating beans every day.

Thank you for helping Mommy feed us for so many days on that one package of beans: beans, bean soup, chili, and potatoes cooked in bean soup.

School starts in a couple of weeks. I really want to ask you for a new dress and pair of shoes, but I can't. We need so many other things...

Good night...

Starting Over

A few days later, while Daddy worked on The Goose, Margaret and I followed Mommy to the Island Creek Coal Company Store. She led us across the railroad tracks, through a narrow ditch and across the paved road.

A group of teens sat on the concrete steps drinking Coke. Several crates of empty pop bottles sat near the store front window along with cartons of sixteen ounce bottles of Coke, Bubble-Up, and Orange Crush. I wanted one, but didn't ask Mommy because I knew we didn't have the money.

Across the aisle was the clothing department. Mommy glanced at the beautiful dresses hanging on racks, the colorful scarves, and jewelry underneath the glass cases. She ran her fingers over a red flowered dress with a matching belt. The clerk asked Mommy if she could help her. Startled, Mommy quickly let go of the dress. She looked down, her cheeks turning red. "Nah, I'm just looking." She switched Noah to her other hip and walked away. I felt sad for her. I wished for once that she could buy something new.

To the left of the clothing department was the grocery section. Mommy checked the price on a package of beans. She sighed. She did the same with a few more items. "We won't be able to shop in here," she said. "They're way too high." Mommy glanced at the hardware, but I lingered near the candy section: boxes of penny candy, cookies, bubble gums, and long pretzel rods lined the shelves behind the counter. A clerk waited on a girl my age. She put a nickel on the counter. "Penny candy, please." The clerk set the box in front of her. She picked out a caramel chew and a red jawbreaker, but I couldn't see what else. Mommy headed for the door. I made my mind up that one day I would earn some money and come back.

August 1st came, and Daddy got our first Welfare check. We were happy, although the money disappeared quickly. Daddy paid rent, bought groceries, and squeezed enough money from it to buy lumber for the bathroom door. He laid four wide boards side by side and placed boards overtop of them making the letter Z. He nailed the top Z boards to the bottom ones. He nailed a handle on the outside of the door and fastened a latch on the inside. It worked fine, and Mommy at last smiled to see that door go up. Although crippled, Daddy could fix almost anything. By the end of the month, though, we were struggling once again for food. When September's check came, Mommy got ready. She wrote the grocery list and pin curled her hair.

"I'm buying curtains today," she told Daddy. "Everyone can see in here." The thought of curtains made me happy, too. I didn't like looking at the dark windows at night, except the one at the end of my bed.

"Go ahead. Don't spend too much."

Daddy let me walk with him to the post office. He showed me how to watch for traffic when I crossed the road, so I could get the mail. The friendly postmaster greeted Daddy and handed him the check. We loaded in the truck and headed to Logan to pay bills. Margaret and I sat in the back as usual. I was fascinated with Logan. It seemed so big. There were no parking spaces left, and the sidewalks were crowded. The utility companies were scattered, so he let Mommy out in front of one so she could go in and pay the bill then circled around, picked her up and drove her to another one. I held Noah and helped Daddy watch for her when it was time to pick her up again. Sometimes we circled two times because of the long lines of people waiting to pay their gas, water, and electric bills.

Once during a trip around the block, heavy traffic on the street forced us to stop in front of the dime store. I looked for Mommy in the steady moving crowd. I didn't see her, but on the street a few feet from me, a blind woman sat on the corner holding a tin cup. Her dark hair was pulled back in a bun, and she wore a blue flowered dress. A basket of small red flowers sat beside her chair. As people passed by, they dropped coins in her cup and spoke to her. I heard "God bless you, Mary" a few times.

On another corner, a man without legs sat on a wooden platform on the pavement. He held a cup, also. The platform had wheels, and I saw him move forward and backward by pushing and pulling himself with two blocks of wood the size of bricks. He was thin and had whiskers. I don't remember anyone calling him by his name as they dropped coins into his cup. I felt sorry for both of them. "Who are they?" I asked.

"Those people have fallen on hard times," Daddy said. Almost like us, I thought. But I looked at them again. The woman had no eyes, and the man had no legs. I changed my mind. Our family wasn't as bad off after all.

After Mommy paid the last bill, Daddy picked her up and dropped her off in front of Sayer Brothers Department store to buy curtains. We circled several times waiting for her. I spotted her on the third time around, but she wasn't in front of Sayer Brothers. "There she is, Daddy." I pointed inside of G.C. Murphy's. Mommy stood in line at the candy counter, and the clerk was handing her a bag. She ran outside and hopped in The Blue Goose before the traffic moved again. She put the curtains in the back and opened the small bag. She gave each of us one chocolate star. I believe Margaret Ann swallowed her piece whole. She held out her hand for more before I had tasted my piece. I let my piece melt slowly, so I could enjoy that chocolate for a long time. Daddy looked at Mommy. "I only got a ¼ pound," she said. "Just a few pieces." She folded the bag and put it in her purse.

"We're gonna be short this month because of the curtains. We didn't need the candy." Daddy said, clearly not happy.

"A treat every once in a while doesn't hurt," Mommy said. She stared ahead through the windshield, clutching her purse tightly. I was glad Mommy got the candy, but I hated when we ran out of money, too!

A&P Supermarket was our last stop. A table filled with dishes, bowls, sheets, and other household items stood near the door. Mommy paused and looked over the items on the table. A clerk approached her. "Ma'am, do you need a book?"

The clerk explained to Mommy how Plaid Stamps were redeemed for gifts. Each page held fifty singles, five rows of ten, or one fifty. Mommy smiled. "How many books for this kitchen bowl?" She pointed to a white mixing bowl with red tulips painted on the sides.

The clerk leafed through a booklet, told her how many she needed, and handed her some books. "Each time you shop, be sure to paste your stamps in these books." Mommy smiled and stuffed the books into her purse. She and Daddy filled their grocery carts, we checked out, and went home.

That evening Mommy hung the curtains. She bought nine pairs of plastic flowered curtains, one pair for each window. They were white with red and yellow bumpy flowers and cost fifty-cents a pair. We couldn't afford curtain rods, so she threaded a white cord through the tops and wrapped the ends around nails pounded into the window frame. She stood back and admired them after they were hung. She also put up more calendars she'd gotten from a funeral home, a bank, and dry cleaners in town. We now had pictures of a little girl praying in church, Jesus knocking on a door, and a pine forest overlooking a green lake. Mommy loved calendars! Maybe she felt like the house was finally a home.

In our neighborhood, the neighbors were kind and always spoke when they passed by. One of them gave us a couple bags of clothes. They came just in time for school. There was a dress for me and a pair of snug fitting shoes that I could wear if I didn't wear socks.

It was September 1959, and I enrolled at Verdunville Grade School. Daddy and Mommy met with the principal. "I'm afraid Katherine will have to repeat first grade," Mr. Gore said. "She was absent too many days last year." Daddy and Mommy agreed.

I didn't mind. The school was beautiful, and I could have lived there. It was a long brick building with a gym, cafeteria, and stage on one end.

There were twelve classrooms—two of each grade—one through six was located on both sides of a long hallway. The floors were clean and polished to a high shine. I thought mashed potatoes could be served on them.

The principal took me to a classroom, introduced me to Mrs. Riddle, my teacher, and gave her my enrollment card. She read it and looked at me. "I see you turned seven a couple of weeks ago." Her whole face lit up when she smiled. I liked her, and I could tell she liked me. During recess, I talked with classmates. Some lived in my neighborhood, and some of them lived across the tracks. It was good having so many kids my age in the same room, unlike the previous school where the kids were different ages. I brought my book list home and gave it to Daddy. He and Mommy made another trip to G.C. Murphy's and bought them. I hated that they had to spend money that we would need for food.

Moving away from Paint Creek was better for me. Mrs. Riddle was kind, and I didn't want to miss a day of school. I loved reading and art. But the best thing was the indoor bathroom. It had a sink, soap, and paper towels. We also had a water fountain. No more outhouses or drinking water from a crock.

Mommy experienced different changes, though. One morning after we moved in, Mommy sat on the porch with her guitar and songbooks. She opened one of the books and strummed. She got the right chords and began to sing. A lady from across the alley walked to our house. Mommy thought she had come to listen to her play and sing.

"Mrs. Evans," she began, "You really know how to play the guitar."

"Thank you," Mommy said with a smile. "Come up and sit down."

"I will later on, but Charles has to sleep right now." Mommy looked at her, her smile fading. "He works third shift and sleeps during the day."

Mommy apologized. No more early morning playing. Back home on Paint Creek, Mommy played any time she had the chance.

One afternoon in October, I came home from school and Daddy and Mommy sat at the kitchen table. "I can't find a tipple or loading dock anywhere that will let me pick up coal scraps," Daddy said.

"If you did, it wouldn't help," Mommy said. "Most houses around here have changed from coal to gas." She diced the last potato and carried the bowl to the stove. We gathered in the kitchen every evening to be near the cook stove. At last, we had heaters in the bedrooms, but to save money, Daddy waited until bedtime to light them. He wanted to keep the gas bill low.

Margaret Ann, almost three, was talking. But she preferred to point and reach to get what she wanted. She reached for Daddy when she wanted to be held, or followed him around, pointed to his leg and said, "Ride pony." Daddy usually gave in unless he was tired. Noah held his bottle pretty good to be eight months old. But now he had learned the game of "I will drop it, and you can pick it up." I got tired of bending over and picking it up for him.

Mommy dumped the potatoes into the hot iron skillet. They sizzled and spat in the hot grease. She salted and peppered them and checked the cornbread in the oven. I loved her fried potatoes. She browned them lightly before turning them. They tasted so good with her crispy cornbread. She didn't complain anymore about the gas stove. She liked striking a match and turning a knob to get fire much better than loading the coal stove on Paint Creek.

Mommy lowered the flame under the potatoes, opened a can of pork and beans, and dumped them into a pot. "We have The Goose to haul scrap iron," Mommy said. "And next summer, there's berry picking."

"That's a long time off. I may have to go to the tipple in Kanawha County and sell a load over there. But it will take half of what I get for gas."

They thought for a minute and Daddy spoke. "We'll stretch the check as far as we can. Rent and groceries come first. We'll figure out something."

By mid-November we were in need again. Daddy and Mommy had hatched a plan.

On a chilly Saturday morning, Daddy put one of our mattresses in the back end of the truck. Mommy gathered several A&P grocery bags. We drove to Holden, a small community not too far away. Daddy parked The Goose at the end of a row of houses and babysat Margaret and Noah as they played on the mattress. Mommy and I went door to door begging for food. Daddy reminded me, "No matter if they give you something or not, you always thank them."

The little community was good to us. We got several cans of food, a package of beans, some noodles and a few dollars. One lady asked us if we were hungry. We nodded and she fixed us peanut butter and crackers and let us eat them on her steps. She made extra for Daddy and Margaret Ann. We got to The Goose just in time. Noah was crying from a dirty diaper, and people came out on their porches to check things out. Daddy pulled out as quickly as he could. He didn't want anyone to think he had harmed the crying baby. I was glad we did not beg in our community where my classmates lived.

When I got up the next Saturday, Daddy sat at the kitchen table cutting old clothes into long pieces. Two large piles lay in the floor. "Whatcha doing," I asked.

"Cutting rags to wrap the pipes outside. I need you to help me."

When he had finished cutting, we carried the rags outside. He walked to the side of the house, took off his peg leg, and laid it on the ground. He shone a flashlight underneath the house and let the light follow the pipes. Then he shone it on the ground and pointed out rocks and bits of wood to avoid. I eyed the dark, dank crawl space warily. But I had to help Daddy, so we crawled under the house and used every rag we had to wrap exposed pipes. It was cold under there and my hands were frozen. Daddy and I were glad to get back into the house.

"Well, that's another thing off the list," he said. "That'll prevent the water from freezing this winter." I was glad that I had helped Daddy with one more job, but I didn't want to go under that house again.

The check came in December, and the rent and utilities were paid and groceries bought once more. By this time, I thought things were getting better. We had a bathroom door, two gas heaters for the bedrooms, curtains, and a repaired roof. I came home from school a few days later, and found Daddy and Mommy sitting at the kitchen table again, discussing bills. I had come to call it "the worry table." That's where they made all our future plans—*for tomorrow.*

"The Goose needs its license. They ran out the last of November. I could get a ticket," Daddy said.

"We barely have enough for food the rest of the month." Mommy placed her head in her hands.

Daddy sipped his coffee. "I'll see what I can do. I'm going to Logan tomorrow."

The next day was Saturday. Daddy did go to Logan like he said. But he came back a short time later. He told Mommy what happened. He sat down on the street to beg in front of G.C. Murphy's. A few minutes later, the Chief of Police told him he could not beg unless he had something to sell or offer the public and that his peg leg took up too much room.

Daddy said he got up, went inside Murphy's, and bought a package of pencils. He returned to his spot only to find the man on the wooden platform had taken his place.

"We can't get ahead," Mommy said, her eyes shiny with tears. "I don't know how much longer I can take this."

"I'll figure out something," Daddy said. He sounded more sure than he looked.

The Murphy's Store where Kathy and her dad sold pencils from the sidewalk.

City Sidewalks

That night it began snowing and by Sunday evening, several inches lay on the ground. The Blue Goose could not venture out because of bald tires. By the following Saturday the roads had improved, and Daddy and I headed out. We drove across the Water Street Bridge, which led into Logan, and turned left onto Middleburg Bridge toward the parking lot on the island. The island was located on the lower end of Logan, surrounded by the Guyandotte River, and was the home of Logan High School and a large public parking lot. Wobbling, pecking pigeons lined the sidewalk. They scattered as we came closer. After we passed, they flew back to the sidewalk and pecked at the pieces of popcorn passersby dropped onto the ground.

A sparkling skiff of snow dusted the ground, and a few lazy flakes floated in the air. The Blue Goose's heater did not work, and the truck was cold. A thin baby blanket covered my lap, and I tucked it tightly beneath my legs. We turned onto the lot.

"Twenty-five cents," said the attendant, holding out her hand. Always, always, someone wanted what little money we had. I concentrated on her booth's pretty decorations. A dark-green wreath with red holly berries hung on the side of the booth and garland draped the door.

Daddy gave the woman a quarter, and she smiled and wiggled her fingers at me. Daddy said parking here was cheaper than a spot in the parking building in town or feeding the storefront meter. Still, it was a long walk through the parking lot and back across the bridge, especially on a cold day.

Daddy turned down the first row of parking slots and drove slowly through more wobbling pigeons. Several spots were empty, but he didn't take any of them. He drove to the edge near the riverside. "We'll take this spot right here," he said. "That way the pigeons won't bother us, and we won't bother them." I nodded, loving how Daddy always realized how important it was to treat even the smallest creatures with respect.

He switched off the motor, turning in the seat to face me. "Now remember," he said, "don't tell 'em you're cold." He always told me that. We didn't want pity. Pity had to be saved for people worse off than we were.

Daddy grabbed his crutches. "No matter who asks, say *no*," he said. "Even if a policeman asks you if you're cold, you say *no*, got it? Because if you say *yes*, they will put me in jail."

I stared out the window as a woman walked down the row in a long, heavy-looking coat that almost touched the ground. She flipped a fluffy red scarf around her neck with gloves that matched her scarf. She buried her nose into the scarf, and I sniffed in a breath. I imagined her scarf must smell like warm bread.

Daddy touched my arm. "Katherine, do you hear me?"

"Yes."

I buttoned my thin coat and grabbed a piece of cardboard from behind my seat. As we crossed the bridge into town, my thoughts turned to the toys I might see in the store windows. The city clock struck 8:45 a.m. as we reached the sidewalk. "Let's hurry," Daddy said. "We need to get to the dime store first." He meant ahead of the blind woman and legless man on the platform. I felt sorry for them, but I realized our family needed money, too.

He tried to walk fast, but it was hard to do with crutches. It was especially difficult for him to maneuver around patches of ice and snow on the sidewalk. He could have walked faster on his peg leg. I didn't understand why the policemen thought it took up too much room.

We passed the bus depot, crossed the railroad tracks, and followed the sidewalk that led into town around a curved building. And there, straight in front of me, was Christmas! Everywhere. In all directions and as far as I could see. Twinkling lights, tinkling bells, brilliant stars, sparkling tinsel, plastic reindeer—and Santa!

"Oh!" For a moment, my mouth forgot how to make words. "How pretty!" I finally managed.

Daddy said nothing. We waited at the intersection for the light to turn, and I gaped at the red, green, and silver decorated storefronts and street corners. A reindeer hung from garland stretched across the street at the stop light, and garland with bells swung from utility poles.

Daddy nudged me when the light changed. "Come on."

The smell of spicy pumpkin pies greeted us before we passed the Nu-Era Bakery. Frosted gingerbread men, Santa-faced cookies, and vanilla fudge lined the window. My mouth watered.

"Not much longer now," he said. "Another block to go." Snowflakes fell like feathers in the air, tickling my nose. I shivered, but I made myself ignore the cold and instead thought of places I'd rather be, like playing with new toys in front a warm fire, or snuggling in a soft, warm bed with plenty of blankets.

A clock chimed. "Nine o'clock," Daddy said. "We made it in time. The clerk is unrolling the awning now." I looked up at the dime store's long red storefront covered with huge gold words: *G.C. Murphy*. I didn't see the blind woman or legless man anywhere in the streets.

The sidewalk in front of the store was vacant. I put down the cardboard for Daddy to sit on, and he sat down in his all-day work position. He tried not to take up much space on the sidewalk, in case the police came back. He placed his good leg and stump as close to him as he could, removed his worn felt hat and placed it on his lap. He tossed in a few pencils from his inside pocket and waited for his first customers. I slid his crutches behind him, out of the way. I hurried inside on the heels of the store clerk to buy another package of pencils, and I ran back out quickly. I didn't want Daddy to run out of pencils.

A little further on the sidewalk, a man unlocked the Salvation Army booth. Within a few minutes, "Silent Night" blared from the booth's speaker. The man placed a red tripod in front of the booth and hung a red kettle in the middle. He walked back and forth in front of the stand, ringing a gold handbell.

Not many people were out yet, so I turned to look at the toy display in the window. In the first window were holsters with six-shooter cap guns, a Daisy BB Gun, a Betsy Wetsy with a bottle tied to her hand, a jack-in-the-box, and a Gene Autry Pistol. A long Flexible Flyer Sled was propped in the corner next to a red Radio Flyer wagon filled with Lincoln Logs, a game of Monopoly, and a musical teddy bear.

The second window displayed a pair of plastic binoculars, a pellet pistol, an orange tea set, several Matchbox cars, a Tiny Tears doll, and behind the doll, a baby bed. Next to it stood an ironing board with a real electric iron—only it was made for little girls like me. I stared at the iron and ironing board. Oh, how I'd love to have that. But my eyes returned to the orange tea set. I imagined myself playing house and pouring tea for my doll at home—a doll with red rooted hair and one blinking eye. I'd found her on the creek bank, and I loved her. Her body was broken, but she was beautiful on the inside, like my Daddy. I sighed.

Within an hour, Daddy and I were almost out of pencils. I went inside to buy more. This time, I didn't hurry. I lingered around the candy counter up front, just tall enough to see into the different sections displaying nuts and candies. Caramels, crème drops, maple goodies, popped corn and hot roasted cashews lay behind the glass. Someday, I thought, I'll walk right up to this counter and order my own chocolate stars. The clerk will weigh them, put them in a crisp, white bag and hand them to me. Someday, it will be *my* turn.

I hurried past the cosmetic counter stacked with bottles of Evening in Paris, tubes of red lipstick, and large, pink powder puffs. I grabbed a pack of pencils from the office supplies rack and carried them to the checkout. On the way out, I passed paper dolls, coloring books, and comic books. *Dennis the Menace* and *Archie* looked like they would be such fun to read!

Daddy had only two pencils left when I got back outside. I dumped more pencils into his hat and stood beside him once more. By this time, the streets were filled with shoppers. Almost everyone stopped at the dime store's window display to look at the toys. I stood and listened as parents asked their children what they wanted Santa to bring. I couldn't imagine being asked that question.

Soon the city clock chimed the noon hour. Daddy searched the coins in his hat. He handed me a quarter and said, "Stir it." He had only done this a couple of times before, but I understood his order. He meant for me to buy a fountain soda and stir it to mix the water and syrup before I took a drink.

I hurried inside, ordered a hotdog and soda from the lunch counter and ate quickly. Everything tastes better when eaten from a lunch counter, I learned—even a plain old hotdog.

After I'd finished eating, it was hard to leave the warm, comfortable stool. Still, I knew I had to return to my spot. I hopped down from the stool and carried my cup outside. I saved the last drink of soda for Daddy. He wouldn't dare eat anything during the day, because he said it didn't look right for him to eat on the street. He always waited until he got home.

I dumped more pencils into his hat. The streets were more crowded than before, and new onlookers stopped to gaze at the toy display. I walked along the display window and stopped in front of the bright orange tea set again. I studied the little teapot, the four little cups, and the matching tray on which they sat. It was about the prettiest thing I'd ever seen.

A woman and a little girl approached the window. The girl stood in front of the dolls and stared at each one.

"Which one do you want Santa to bring?" the woman asked.

"I want Betsy Wetsy," the little girl said.

The woman turned and looked at me. "And what do you want, sweetheart?"

I ducked my head but peered up at her, feeling my cheeks warm. "The tea set." I didn't know if I'd said it loud enough for her to hear.

"Well, let's go tell Santa." The woman took her daughter's hand, and they went inside the store.

I watched after them a bit, the door closing. Suddenly, I noticed I'd been stepping side to side and back and forth as cold stabbed at my feet. It felt like ants crawled on them. I stomped a few times, trying to make the tingling go away, but it didn't help. I peered up at a faint sun, which did nothing to warm me. It was late afternoon. Cheery shoppers stepped around me as they carried huge packages to their cars and hurried off to do more shopping.

A few times, shoppers dropped coins into Daddy's hat, wished us a Merry Christmas, and didn't take any pencils. "Merry Christmas, and God bless you," Daddy said each time.

Shoppers hurried up and down the street. By afternoon, things slowed down. People piled into their cars and headed out of town. As the clock chimed the hour, Daddy said, "That's it. We're finished." He handed me the remaining pencils, counted the coins in his hat, dropped them into a black sock and held it up toward me.

"Did we get enough," I asked.

Daddy smiled. "There's enough for the truck license and a few groceries, too." He tied the end of the sock and put it into his pocket.

I was cold and tired, but I knew Daddy must be even colder. He had sat on the cold concrete all day, wearing only a thin pair of pants, a thin coat, and nothing on his head.

I helped him stand up and placed the crutches under his arms. He stood for a few seconds to get the blood flowing in his good leg, and as I turned to pick up the cardboard, a bright and cheery voice said, "Merry Christmas!"

I pulled a pencil out of my bag thinking someone wanted to buy one. When I turned, I was surprised to see the woman who'd been at the display window. She bent down, hugged me, and placed a package in my hand.

I peeked inside—*the tea set!* I opened the bag wider to let Daddy see. He smiled at the woman, and he opened his mouth to say something, but he closed it again. He nodded and smiled.

"Thank you! Merry Christmas," I said and she walked away. I hugged the tea set against my chest and watched as the woman quickly disappeared around the corner. I turned to Daddy and grinned.

Daddy's eyes were wet. He smiled at me, but his lips quivered when he did.

He was happy I had gotten the tea set—he was always happy for me. I knew that. So why did he look so sad? I gripped the package and cardboard tightly and headed down the street with Daddy.

One block below G. C. Murphy's, the blind woman sat in a chair. Red paper flowers sat at her feet, and a silver cup in her hand. When we passed by, Daddy dropped some coins into her cup. "Merry Christmas, Mary!" he said.

Christmas

Mrs. Riddle put up a Christmas tree and our class made decorations. We pasted strips of red and green construction paper together to make a paper chain and strung it on the tree. I was proud to place my string on the tree with the others. Our school had a Christmas program, and each class sang a couple of songs on the stage. I don't remember what two songs we sang, but I liked doing it.

Mrs. Riddle let us draw names, but I didn't because we had no extra money. On the day of the party, I watched other kids open gifts and remembered my little doll, tea set, and Big Ben. At least Margaret and I had something to play with. I also watched Mrs. Riddle open several gifts from the students. I will never forget all the Christmas corsages she got and what she did with each one. She opened them one at a time, thanked the student, and described it to the class as she pinned it on her blouse.

It went something like this.

"Oh my! Billy, what a beautiful gold-glittered pinecone with matching gold ribbon." She wore it for a few minutes and opened another one. "Diana, thank you for the beautiful blue-glittered bells with such a pretty silver ribbon and pearls!" She took off Billy's and put on Diana's for a few minutes. There was Ronnie's present, too. "Ronnie, look at that precious tiny snowman sitting on a sprig of pine all circled in a shiny red ribbon." She put it on and took turns all afternoon wearing each corsage for several minutes, making the gift giver feel special.

I liked how she took time to carefully describe the gifts to the class, and I wished I had one to give her. One thing I was determined to do the next year; I would draw names with the others, and I would buy my teacher a gift.

There was no Christmas tree at home and no presents, but I was happy that Daddy used some of the money from begging to buy a few apples and oranges. He bought extra sugar and nuts for Mommy to make her special fudge. She cut it into squares and hid it in a coffee can behind the refrigerator. We couldn't wait until she wiggled the refrigerator away from the wall and gave us a piece. It was delicious.

One of the coal miners in the camp bought a new living room suite for his family for Christmas, and he gave us his old set. We put the green sofa and chair in the living room with the gas heater and Philco radio. Mommy was happy that she had a place to play her guitar and listen to the Grand Ole Opry.

Mommy told Daddy she couldn't sleep with two growing kids, and Daddy said he couldn't sleep with me because I was getting too big to sleep at the foot of the bed. He said I kicked him in the face while I was dreaming. A week or so later, Daddy bought a used half bed for me and put it in Mommy's bedroom. I was so thrilled to have my own bed. I had him place it along the wall near a window where I could see the night sky.

Now Mommy slept with ten-month-old Noah, and two-and-a-half-year-old Margaret slept at the foot of Daddy's bed. I was happy to have my own bed at seven-and-a-half, but I wished Margaret and I could have gotten some clothes and toys, too. Daddy said the furniture, heater, and license for the truck were good presents for him, and Mommy seemed happy that she had furniture for the living room and a warm heater to sit near. For a change, things seem to be getting better.

Near the end of December, I went to get the mail. While I was in line, I noticed people looking at their mail and throwing some of it away in a small wooden barrel beside the door. Someone missed the barrel and their magazine landed on the floor beside it. It said, *Earn Your Own Money*. I picked it up and glanced through the pages. When I saw what was on the inside, I took it home to show Mommy and Daddy.

Pictures of assorted ink pens, letter openers, and desk sets crammed the pages and described how you could earn money by selling them. They studied the ink pen sets and desk sets. Mommy especially liked the gold Jesus attached to a white pearly cross. "We need to order some of these to sell. I know people'll like them," Mommy said.

They flipped through more pages. "We're gonna need extra money for roach spray, wallpaper, not to mention the higher gas bills this winter," Mommy said. I really wanted the roach spray more than anything. When we thought we'd killed them all, the remainder had been in hiding. There were so many, and they were everywhere. I had knocked one off my blanket the previous night, and Mommy still washed every dish and pot before she used it. I couldn't wait until we got rid of them. I wasn't afraid of roaches because I'd grown up with them, but I hated them and wanted them gone forever.

Daddy turned a few more pages. "These ink pens with letter openers attached on the end are beautiful. It says they come with a picture of John F. Kennedy on one side and Mother Mary on the other side."

I peeked over his shoulder. Each pen was about the size of a pencil, and the bottom of the ink pen was black. The top half was clear plastic and narrowed into a sharp plastic point, and inside the clear plastic was a picture of a woman with a blue scarf around her head and a red heart in front of her chest. "Who is that woman," I asked.

"That is Mother Mary of the bleeding heart," Mommy said. "Jesus' mother."

I studied the picture some more and looked at the man whose picture was on the other side of the letter opener. He wore a blue suit and tie and combed his hair to one side. He looked important. I pointed to the picture. "Who's that?"

"John Kennedy. He might run for President," Daddy said.

"I bet those would sell," Mommy said.

I had never seen Mommy or Daddy get so excited before. I was glad I had brought the magazine home. The thought of them having extra money made me happy. I didn't like that Daddy begged on the street, or that we went door to door and begged for food. Maybe this was meant for us to do.

Daddy flipped over a few more pages. "Here's the order form."

"What about the Welfare?" Mommy said. "We don't want them to cut off our check again." She leaned back in her chair and folded her arms. "I won't go through that again."

Daddy flipped through the pages once more. "Let me think on it some," Daddy said. "Put it away for now."

Mommy laid the magazine on top of the refrigerator. She only put important mail up there. This meant she was serious. The look in her eyes told me she would find a way to buy those ink pens. She had gone without too much for too long.

I didn't want our family to get in trouble with Welfare again, but I sure hoped things would get better and stay better in 1960. The New Year was only a day away.

Winter of 1960

The New Year came and brought colder temperatures. Cold air sneaked in the usual places—underneath doors, cracks in the floors, and windowsills. I chose to sleep at the foot of my new bed, pull back the curtain, and watch the moon rise, even though cold air rushed through the broken panes and rotted frames.

Daddy hadn't been able to underpin the house, and the inside never reached a warm temperature unless the heaters were on high. This meant higher gas bills. The walls and windows sweated, even dampening Mommy's calendars that had Jesus pictured in various poses. Every time she went to town, she picked up a few more. We now had a collection on every wall in every room. I always wondered if Jesus cared about me.

I wiped the windows down with a rag at night and watched the snow fall. I buried beneath the rough patch quilt and only let my eyes peek out because the cold froze my nose.

Snows came and went, January turned into February, but I still climbed the hill to school every day. I loved learning, school, and my classmates. Besides, the school was nice and warm when I got there.

There was one thing that could make things perfect. I waited for the day that Daddy could give me a quarter to buy my lunch in the cafeteria. I imagined the cooks handing me a tray with meatloaf, mashed potatoes, and peas and carrots. I couldn't ask him for more money, so I kept on eating my jelly sandwich for lunch every day and buying milk with the three cents he gave me. I knew that the day would come when I'd get that quarter.

One cold day I came home from school and found Mommy doing laundry in the kitchen. Last month she'd asked Daddy to move the Maytag inside because it was too cold to wash on the porch. The washer squeaked and strained as it churned the clothes, and her large washtub sat in a chair filled with rinse water. Water droplets covered the floor, and the kitchen smelled of soap and bleach. We walked carefully in the kitchen to avoid falling on the slippery linoleum. A pot of beans cooked on the stove, and Mommy asked me to salt them. I carefully measured a teaspoon and dumped them into the beans. I remembered the time I accidentally over-salted them and didn't want that to happen again.

Daddy pulled in and blew the horn. I opened the door to see what he wanted. "I need help carrying in," he said.

Daddy had a few boxes of commodities he'd gotten from a church up the road. We got a few cans of beef, a long loaf of cheese, a few pounds of butter, a large can of peanut butter, a box of powdered milk, and a few cans of powdered eggs. It was Christmas all over again!

"All of this came at the right time," Mommy said. "We need every bit."

"Yeah, and make sure you wrap up whatever you open or be sure to put it in the refrigerator," Daddy said. "Roaches are getting real bad. We'll spray again as soon as it warms up and we can open the doors and windows." I didn't want to spoil their good day, but I had seen a tiny roach in the refrigerator last night. I knocked it onto the floor and stepped on it. I couldn't wait for warmer weather.

Meanwhile, we enjoyed melted cheese on toast under the oven broiler and warmed beef and powdered scrambled eggs for breakfast. Mommy was glad that Noah ate table food because it helped cut down on buying so much milk. Our family loved peanut butter, but I didn't understand why it came with an inch or more of oil on top. Mommy worked hard to mix the oil into the peanut butter to make it easier to spread, but usually it tore the bread anyway. But we were still thankful.

This food helped us get by, especially since Daddy wasn't able to search for scrap iron due to the weather.

After we put away the groceries, I helped Mommy hang our wet clothes on lines in the bedroom. Daddy strung rope across the room in several directions and nailed the ends to the tops of door frames and windows. Even though Mommy put the clothes through the Maytag's wringer, water still dripped from the clothes. There were puddles of water all over the bedroom floor, and we had to keep mopping it up. It was hard to walk to the bathroom because of all the wet clothes hanging throughout the room. I did not like brushing up against them.

As I mopped, I remembered what Mommy told me about her life as a little girl. Her mother died when she was five, leaving her and two brothers. Her father married a woman with two kids, and later, he died, too. Every day the stepmother made her mop the floors, clean the house, and wash clothes like in the fairytale *Cinderella*. Mommy's brothers ran away and joined the navy, and she left home too. Mommy said she struggled being on her own for a few years before she met and married Daddy, who was already struggling to live with one hand and one leg. It didn't seem like things were much better for her or Daddy.

"Turn the gas heaters up high in every room," Mommy said. "The heat will dry them."

"We can, but it will make the gas bill go higher," Daddy said. The clothes dripped, and we mopped. By bedtime, the clothes were partially dry.

So far, our family had made it through the winter without any colds or flu. But I guess somebody had to take a turn, and it was me. That evening, I let out a cough or two. Daddy seemed concerned. I was worried. Usually, he made cough syrup every winter by boiling pancake syrup and dropping in a few drops of cinnamon oil, and a few other spices. After it cooled, he stored it into a Mason jar and sealed it tight. If I had a chest cold, he gave me a half teaspoon of Vicks VapoRub to swallow, or made a Musterole plaster for my chest. But he didn't make any this winter, and I hadn't seen the other items on the bathroom shelf.

Before bed, Daddy looked outside and checked the doors. "It's snowing again," he said. He turned the gas heaters to low, while I slipped into the kitchen for water. I took a long drink to help push any cough way down, making sure it couldn't come out, and I climbed into my half bed across from Mommy. She and Noah were already asleep. My throat felt funny, and I felt the urge to cough, but I wouldn't let it.

I didn't like the feel of the stiff patchwork quilt Mommy made from old coats and jeans. It was rough, but I stuffed a corner of it into my mouth to block the cough. I kept my head under the covers, ignoring the wooly taste and the tickling in my throat. It was hard to breathe, but no matter how hard that cough tried to come out, I fought to keep it in.

I faced the window to further muffle any cough that might sneak out, but cold air rushed past my head, forcing me to turn over. Now I faced Daddy's bedroom. The quilt corner became wet from my spit, my nose burned, and my eyes watered. I was going to lose. I could not silence my cough any longer. I spit out the quilt, covered my mouth, and coughed long and hard. I hoped no one heard me.

"Kathy, is that you coughing?" Daddy asked through the open door.

"Yes."

"Get to the kitchen."

Oh, no! Not the kitchen. I remembered a couple of home remedies Daddy used when there was no cough medicine. Which one would he use this time?

The bed springs squeaked as he sat up and moved around. The string from the light socket hung in the center of the room, its end dangling about two feet from the ceiling. He found it and tugged. The light came on.

I moved the curtains back a little to look at the new-fallen snow. The white-blanketed alley glistened beneath the corner streetlight. Moisture ran down the inside of the window. I pulled the curtains back and wrote "No!" on one of the sweaty panes. Another cough slipped out.

"Kathy, did you hear me?" Daddy asked.

"Yes. I'm getting up now." I threw the quilt back and climbed out of bed. The linoleum floor felt like ice. No insulation. No scatter rugs.

I walked to the kitchen and felt in the dark for the light cord hanging over the kitchen table. I tugged, and the light from the bright bulb dangling from the ceiling hurt my eyes. I cupped my hands to my mouth. Another deep cough rushed out.

"Bring me a spoon, Kathy," Daddy said. "Salt and pepper, too."

"Okay." I opened the spoon drawer. Roaches scattered, but I was too worried to chase them. *What home remedy was I gonna get this time?*

I searched through the silverware, found a spoon and grabbed the salt and pepper shakers from the kitchen table. I carried them to Daddy. He sat on the edge of his bed, as I had seen him do so many times before. I wished we had cough syrup or cough drops, but I already knew the answer to that wish.

"Hold the spoon straight," he said. "Don't let it tip over."

I held the teaspoon and watched as he sprinkled a good dose of salt into its bowl. Next, he sprinkled on a generous dose of pepper.

"All right," he said. "Swallow it down."

I put the spoon to my mouth and took all of it at once. My mouth hated the grainy, salty-hot taste. I wanted to spit it out, but I knew better.

"Did you swallow it?" he asked.

"I'm trying," I strangled out, my tongue thick with a crust of salt and pepper.

"Swallow it down and get a drink of water." He handed me the salt and pepper shakers.

The pepper burned my throat as I swallowed, but I didn't say a word. I placed the salt and pepper shakers on the table, dropped the spoon into the sink, and searched through the jars in the sink. I found a nearly clean, pint-sized Mason jar. I rinsed it, ran about an inch of water from the faucet and took one drink, careful not to drink more. I wanted to drink a whole jar full, but I knew better. Daddy had told me many times that if I drank more than one swallow, the cough remedy would not work. I guess I wanted it to work as bad as he did.

He turned off his light and settled back under his covers. I made my way back to the bedroom in the dark. I climbed into bed quietly, so I would not wake Mommy or Noah. I waited for the cough to come, and sure enough, it did. It began building deep in my throat. My mouth wanted to open so badly and cough long, hard, deep, and loud. I would not let it. I stuffed the sheet into my mouth. *I will not cough.* Another coughing spell would bring with it another home remedy. Next time, it might be Texas Pete's Hot Sauce.

My cough continued throughout the night and into the next day, but Daddy didn't try any more of his home remedy. That afternoon, I had a fever, sore throat, and chills. Daddy took me to see a doctor in Logan. We parked on the island near Logan High School and walked into town. The doctor's office was upstairs between two stores along Stratton Street. Daddy walked up the stairs sideways, maneuvering one leg at a time as he held onto both walls. He positioned himself carefully to climb the steps, and it was slow, difficult, and likely painful. By the time he reached second floor, Daddy was winded and could barely catch his breath.

The words *Enter—Come In* were written on the opaque glass of the doctor's office. Inside, several leather chairs with deep sinkholes from broken springs and overuse lined the walls. The small waiting room was crowded. Another opaque glass read *Doctor's Office.* Every few minutes, the doctor opened the door to let out a patient, and said, "Next!" He had no receptionist or patient-numbering system. No one argued or disagreed about whose turn it was. We paid attention to who was there before us, and who came in after us. We knew when it was our turn to get up and go.

Other than an occasional child crying behind the closed door, the only sounds were the doctor asking, "How are you today?" or "What's wrong?" as he closed his office door.

The patient said something, and the muffled words were cut off by the closing door. Silence. Moments later, the door opened, the patient walked out, and the doctor said, "Next!"

It was our turn. Daddy and I entered the doctor's office, and the doctor closed the door. He wore a jacket and pants and had white hair with grey streaks. A brown desk with nothing on the top sat on the right side of the room beside a tall, white cabinet with glass doors and drawers along the bottom. A leather-covered bed sat near the opposite wall. "What's wrong?" he asked Daddy.

"She's sick," Daddy started, but the doctor had already ignored him.

Without waiting for an explanation, the doctor opened a door on the cabinet and pulled out a small bottle and syringe. "Roll up your sleeve," he said to me. He stabbed the needle into my arm. Next, he grabbed a small, white, pill envelope, opened a large brown bottle, and dumped in several white pills. He scribbled on the outside, "Take three a day."

Before I could nod, he'd already turned away from me.

As I put on my coat, the doctor opened the door.

"Next!"

When I got home my head hurt, and I went to bed, but I heard Mommy and Daddy talking in the kitchen. "What did the doctor say?" Mommy asked.

"Not much."

"Well, what does she have?"

"He didn't say. Gave her a shot and this packet of pills."

"That's a Welfare doctor for ya. They don't care," Mommy sighed.

I wasn't sure I understood what she meant by calling him a *Welfare* doctor. I knew she blamed the Welfare for cutting off our check for selling coal. I knew they were the reason we had to move, and I knew the Welfare sent investigators to your home to see how you lived and what you had. But what did she mean about him not caring?

Democrat Rally

I was 7 ½ years old in the spring of 1960 when Daddy and Mommy drove to Logan to hear a new politician. We left early to get a close parking spot. Daddy stayed in the truck with one-year-old Noah while Mommy led me and Margaret across the street to the courthouse where the young man was scheduled to speak. From where Daddy parked, he could hear the speech with the windows rolled down.

Mommy edged her way through the crowd to get closer to the flatbed truck where the speaker stood. Robert Kennedy finished his speech and started for the steps. Mommy grabbed our hands and ran toward him. She told him we were hungry and our Welfare check wasn't enough to keep us fed. He opened his wallet and handed her a twenty dollar bill. Mommy smiled and tears filled her eyes. She shook his hand and said, "Thank you and God bless you!"

She pressed through the crowd and hurried to The Goose. Mommy proudly waved the twenty dollar bill in front of Daddy. "Let's go to the A & P!" she said.

"Hmm. That Kennedy fellow must be a good man after all," Daddy said.

"Was that the man on the letter opener?" I asked.

As we drove to the A&P on the outside of town, Daddy explained that the man was Robert Kennedy, brother of John F. Kennedy. John, running for President, was on the letter opener.

A few minutes later, Daddy pulled in the parking lot, and we went inside. Mommy stopped in front of the glass case that held gifts for

Plaid Stamp redemptions. The mixing bowl with red tulips sat between a shiny white mixer and a set of flowered drinking glasses. She stared at it, grinned a little, and pulled a cart from the line. I knew she wanted it badly. I followed them through the store as Mommy checked off things on her list. At the checkout, she was excited when the clerk gave her more Plaid Stamps. She counted them to make sure he gave the correct amount before putting them in her purse.

Sometime later, we were low on food again. When we learned there was another, larger rally scheduled at Logan High School's indoor stadium, we packed in The Blue Goose and parked on Middleburg Island near the school, in case luck would befall us and food would appear.

Inside the noisy field house, Daddy paused for a moment. He took a quick look around. "The tables are over there." He pointed to the left. "Follow me."

People moved steadily and pushed us away from the door and farther inside the already-crowded room. We followed closely behind Daddy as he led us underneath red, white, and blue pleated banners draped along balcony railings. Overhead, posters with pictures of smiling men and women hung from the ceiling rafters. "Kennedy for President," the largest one read. "Vote Democrat All The Way."

Now on all sides, people wore buttons pinned to dresses and shirt collars that read, "Justice for Sheriff." White paper hats trimmed with red and blue read, "Barron for Governor." Some adults shouted and waved signs in the air.

Daddy's eyes searched through the thick blanket of people. "There it is." He pointed to the left side of the stage. "Come on. It's over there."

Once more, we made our way through the crowd, following closely behind Daddy. His words burned in my ears. "Now you kids be sure and eat all you can. It's there for you. Fill your bellies full. Anyone who goes home hungry, it's their own fault."

I stared at the line of twenty or so tables filled with nothing but mounds and mounds of food. Two women arrived with stacks of white cardboard plates. Lines quickly formed on both sides of the tables.

"Come on," Daddy said. "Get in line. Don't drop your plates. Hold 'em real tight. Remember now, eat till you're full."

I stared at the tables of food that stretched from one end of the building to the other. Men and women in line ahead of me talked and laughed. They stacked their plates with fried chicken, baked beans, and potato salad. Finally, they stopped in front of the trays at the end of the tables. They piled on slices of garlic bologna, pimento cheese, and pickles.

"Get your drinks over there," Daddy said, pointing toward a man filling paper cups with RC Cola. The man worked quickly, squeezing pop from a nozzle into lines of empty paper cups. We each took a cup and followed Daddy to metal chairs set up in the far corner of the field house. We placed the plates on our laps and our drinks on the floor.

Tall men in dark suits sat in cushioned chairs on the stage and whispered. Others unwrapped cords and placed microphones on long silver rods. Finally, the speakers blared. "Testing. One. Two."

"Make sure you go back for seconds," Daddy said. "There's plenty over there."

After a while, the lines thinned out. Everyone settled down to eat. Several hundred or so people sat on folding chairs in the middle of the floor. Others ate on the balcony.

The men on the stage took turns speaking into the microphones. The audience clapped and cheered. Sometimes the people stood and waved signs and pictures. I never understood what the men said into the microphones, but Mommy and Daddy kept saying, "That's right. That's absolutely right." And every time a speaker on stage said, "Kennedy is who we need for our next President," the crowd stood up, clapped, and yelled louder.

People huddled and talked in every corner. Others sat at tables and handed out white pamphlets. Some visited the food tables over and over. The cooks kept busy filling the pots and pans.

Mommy and Daddy got comfortable listening to the speeches. I went back to the table, placed two chicken legs on a paper plate, and walked slowly to the back of the field house and out the door. I walked and walked until I found our rusted out Blue Goose, opened the door, and slid the plate under the front seat. I went to the food tables again, each time removing several more chicken legs, each time taking them to the truck and putting them under the front seat. I returned to my parents who were still listening to the speeches, not noticing me.

Next, I went to the booth where the man filled cups with RC Cola. I grabbed two cups and walked to the back of the field house again and out the door to The Goose. I emptied the RC into an empty coffee can Daddy used to fill the radiator. I returned to the field house and stood near the back wall, watched and listened. Minutes later, I walked over to the RC booth, took two more cups and went to the truck again. I repeated this several more times until the coffee can was full. I went back inside and sat beside my parents. I was glad I had gotten some food to take home.

That night we did have full bellies, but the RC tasted funny. Daddy tasted it. "Pour it out. It's gone bad." I dumped it in the sink, rinsed the can, and returned it to The Goose.

I was disappointed, too, because I worked hard filling that can.

Later that night, Daddy and Mommy talked at the kitchen table. They flipped through the little magazine I had brought home from the Post Office back in December. They stared at the Kennedy letter openers. Daddy tore out the order form and began writing.

Entertainment

School ended and Mrs. Riddle gave each of us a big hug and wished us a safe and happy summer. I was excited that I was promoted to the second grade, and I couldn't wait. June brought warmer temperatures and roach spray. We opened doors and windows and sprayed in every room. I hated the smell, but I knew it had to be done. We still saw them but not as bad. I even killed a couple under Big Ben, who still needed painted. Hopefully this summer I could get some paint for him. But for now we were so happy we made it through a harsh winter in our new house and were looking forward to happier times.

Late afternoon after spraying for roaches, Mommy washed and pin curled her hair and took her guitar and songbooks to the front porch. She practiced a new song I had never heard her sing before. It was about everybody going out and having fun—*but not the singer* because he was lonesome. I think it was called *Lonesome Me*. Later, we joined her on the porch.

From the time I was knee-high, our front porch set the stage for entertainment, Appalachian style. When the evening shadows crept down the hills and the lightning bugs flashed, Mommy and Daddy provided the entertainment.

Sometimes Mommy told haint stories—ghost stories—about her relatives in Kentucky or West Virginia. She'd also tell strange tales that her father had passed down. No matter what kind of tale she told, I'd lift my dangling feet off the edge of the porch and scoot closer to her and

Daddy. Her stories captured my imagination.

I will never forget the story she called "The Little Red Demon" that she told the last time we were on the porch. She said that when she was a little girl her mother took her to the wake of a close family member. Back then, neighbors removed furniture from a room in the deceased's house and scrubbed it good. The funeral home brought in the casket and set up folding chairs for visitors. Friends and neighbors brought lots of food and filled the kitchen table and counters. People took turns "sitting up" with the corpse.

At this particular funeral, Mommy said that whenever she went to view the corpse, a little red demon appeared at the head of the casket and fanned her away. This happened every time she tried to go near. Everyone else viewed the corpse whenever they wanted. Mommy was glad when her mother finally told her they were leaving.

I thought about that story long and hard, and I dreamed of that little demon for several nights. Maybe the story meant to always be good or a little demon would get you. I decided I didn't want to hear about it again.

That evening flies swarmed around the screen door. It had been hot all week, and the air was stuffy. Our single window fan did the best it could, but it wasn't enough. I sat close to Mommy because I liked the way her hair smelled sweet and soapy after a shampoo. Margaret and Noah sat on her other side.

"Flies on a screen means it's gonna rain," Daddy said. He swatted one with a flyswatter, and it fell onto the porch. He flipped it into the yard with the swatter. "See those stars up there behind the Williamsons' house?" Daddy asked. He pointed high above the house. "That's the Big Dipper, Katherine. See the four corner stars in his dipper and the stars lined up in the handle?"

"It's upside down," I said.

"That's another sign of rain," Daddy said.

"The air's not moving at all," Mommy said. "It's gonna take a big wind to blow in rain tonight." She finished her last song as the evening shadows settled between the hills of Mud Fork, and now she leaned her guitar against the porch wall and slid her songbook under the glider. She sat still—Daddy, too. Mommy and Daddy had shared stories about relatives before, but I never heard them mention too many about their parents.

"Tell us about your parents," I said. "Would we have liked them?"

Mommy spoke first. "I don't remember my mother, but you would have loved Poppa Tony." She laughed. "He'd hurry through the house and speak that language from the old country—Italy—where he was born. He never got to see any of you." I imagined him with his handlebar mustache playing his accordion on his front porch.

Daddy swatted a fly and leaned back in his rocker. "I never knew my parents at all, only what relatives told me about 'em. They died when I was real young, and I stayed in several different homes until I was sixteen." He looked at me. "Kathy, you favor the picture I have of my mother—brown eyes and hair and high cheekbones." There it was. My grandparents were dead, and we would never know their love. Maybe that is why Mommy and Daddy never hugged us or each other. No one showed them how.

"Let me tell ya'll a story," Mommy said.

"Yeah, and make it scary," Margaret added.

I held my breath, hoping, anticipating, practically praying for the story that might follow.

Mommy adjusted two bobby pins in the front of her hair and looked at us. It was as if she read our faces, trying to decide what level of scare she wanted to deliver. She stood and walked to the end of the porch. She peered around the back of the house and did the same at the other end of the porch, as if making sure the secrets she was about to relay wouldn't be overheard by those who didn't want their secrets disclosed.

Daddy never said a word, but he watched her and puffed on his cigarette.

"What are you looking for?" my sister asked.

"Making sure nothing's out there," she said. "I've been wantin' to tell this one for a while, but I had to wait for the right time. I believe tonight's the night."

It sounded like a good one was on the way, so Margaret and I hustled to get closer. She handed Noah to Daddy and sat down on the glider. "Scoot over and give me some room," she said.

"Several years ago, a cousin of mine, Anna, got married and moved to Kentucky." Mommy's soft voice remained low and steady. "She and her husband moved into a little house at the head of a holler. A small washhouse sat at the edge of the fence, near a little creek."

The first breeze of the evening blew in from the alley, and despite the chill in the air, we stayed put. Except for the faint glow from a streetlight several houses away, it was dark on the porch—too dark to make out faces, only forms. We could tell if someone moved or turned a head, but little else.

"The washhouse was kinda located in a dark spot on the property, surrounded by lots of trees." Mommy's hands drew trees in the air. "Anna said she hated going down there to wash, because something didn't feel right down there. It felt like someone was watching her."

Daddy tossed his cigarette butt in the yard, and now I couldn't see the outline of his face glowing in the orange light from the end of the cigarette. I couldn't see his face at all, and I shivered.

"When they moved in," Mommy continued, "a neighbor told them the washhouse was haunted. He said a man escaped from the insane asylum, crossed the mountain, and hung himself in the washhouse."

The wind picked up a little, reminding me that I was alive. It felt good. All the windows were open, and it satisfied me to know that hot air was being pushed out of the house. We would sleep better.

Mommy stood.

"Where ya goin'?" Margaret asked. Her voice quavered.

"I'm finishing the story," Mommy said.

A lightning bolt lit up the sky on the other side of the hill.

"Wow! That was bright," Daddy said. "Storm's moving this way."

Mommy stared into the darkness as she spoke, and I wondered if she was seeing the past or looking for whatever might be listening out there. "Anna said that one evening, she started toward the washhouse to bring in the clothes she'd hung on the line. As she stepped off the back porch and onto the path leading to the washhouse, the little building rose about a foot off its foundation and sat back down."

In the near dark, Mommy's form stood in front of us, facing the alley, as if she were pointing toward the little building.

"She rubbed her eyes," Mommy continued, "because she thought they were playing tricks. The washhouse rose again, and this time she saw the dead man underneath it with his hands raised high." Mommy raised her hands in the air like she was holding up something.

"He began twirling the washhouse around and around, like this." Mommy turned around and around, keeping her hands in the air. "After several spins, he laid it back down where it was before." I squeezed Daddy's arm.

"Mommy, stop!" Margaret said.

A bolt of lightning laced through the sky, followed by a clap of thunder. A strong wind blew across the porch and through the open windows. The plastic curtains flapped hard in the wind, and a calendar fell off the wall.

"That's about it for tonight," Daddy said. "We'd better get inside." Rain drops splattered on the roof and blew onto the porch. "I need to roll up the truck windows."

Another lightning bolt struck something on the other side of the mountain. The alley lit up. Mommy jumped up and grabbed Noah. "Get my guitar, Kathy." She ran inside.

"You kids get off that porch now, before you get struck by lightning," she said from inside the door.

We ran inside as a hard downpour raged outside. Lightning flashed all around our little coal camp and seemed to bounce from hill to hill. The back door opened and slammed from the wind, so I ran through the house and locked it. I hurried to close the open windows to prevent the sheets of driving rain from blowing inside. Margaret and Noah were in the living room with Daddy, watching the water run down the alley.

"Kathy!" Mommy called from the back of the house. "Help me! Hurry!"

I found her in the bathroom standing over the washbowl. "What's wrong?"

"Help me get these bobby pins out of my hair, before I get struck by lightning!" A sob softened her voice. She yanked bobby pins from the sides and top of her head, so I started in the back. In no time, we had them all out. Mommy looked at me tearfully, thankfully. I never thought of bobby pins as lightning rods, and it both frightened me and made me proud that I might have saved her life.

I joined everyone at the front door. Daddy had propped it open a crack so we could see.

After a while, the lightning stopped, and the storm calmed down. Daddy opened a couple of windows, and a fresh, rain-scented breeze blew through the house. A soft, steady rain fell in the foggy alley, and suddenly I felt drowsy. I meandered through the house until I found Mommy lying on the bed, sound asleep with her Bible spread open on her chest. She held her father's rosary in her hand.

Had she been praying? I'd only seen her bow her head and whisper. I never heard the words she spoke except the time a little girl in the camp cut her foot on a tin can. Her mother sent for Mommy, and she ran out of the house with a white dish rag. I ran after her and stood close beside her. She pressed the white cloth on the bloody foot and began, "God bless Mother Mary that ever gave the sweetest milk ..." She stopped and pushed me back with her elbow when she realized I was listening. "You can't hear this," she said and continued praying. The bleeding stopped immediately. Although I asked her later, she refused to tell me the words to the *special* prayers that she spoke when someone had gotten cut or burned.

I didn't understand. Why had the storm frightened her so bad? Was something else bothering her?

Later that night, when the house settled, I listened to everyone's slow breathing. Daddy's low whisper reached my ears. "Lord, have mercy on me, a sinner."

I wondered why he said that.

Black Gold

Near the middle of July Daddy came home excited. He laid a handful of blackberries on the table. "They're in," he said. "Time to go pickin'."

I popped one in my mouth. It was sweet and juicy. "I'm ready," I said. "I'll get the buckets and pans."

"Get your boots and extra clothes, too."

Daddy loved blackberry picking time. Not only were they good to eat, they sold good too. People baked them in pies and cobblers and used them to make jelly and jam for winter.

Mommy was singing "O Lonesome Me" but put down the guitar and made a store list when she heard we were going after berries. She handed it to me, and Daddy and I were on our way to his favorite berry-picking territory.

Daddy pulled into the gas station in Logan and turned off the motor. He dumped the coins from his change purse into my hands. "Put two dimes and two nickels on the dash," he said. I found the coins quickly and put them on the flat space above the glove box.

"How much is left?"

I counted the few remaining coins. "There's a dollar," I said. "Exactly one dollar." I handed the money back to him.

"Can I help you?" asked the station attendant.

"Give me a dollar's worth of ethyl." Daddy handed him the correct amount of coins I'd counted out, and he put the dimes and the nickels I'd placed on the dash back into his coin purse. I watched out the window as the attendant pumped the gas. When he finished, Daddy maneuvered the steering wheel, while I helped with the gas stick. We pulled out of the lot and headed to the end of town, where we turned left at the intersection and picked up Route 52 toward the Kentucky state line.

When we arrived, a line of vehicles waited to cross the toll bridge into Kentucky. The Blue Goose pulled into line. I leaned on the dashboard, peering out the dusty windshield. "I don't see anyone in the booth, Daddy." I turned to him and grinned hopefully. "Maybe today is a free day."

The sign posted on the outside of the tollbooth bore large block letters.

TOLL FEES
Car & Driver.............10 cents
Truck & Driver..........15 cents
Each Passenger..........05 cents

"Here, Kathy." He handed me his change purse. "Get out a dime and a nickel and climb into the back."

I dug in his coin purse purposefully, though it wasn't hard to find the two coins, since there were only four. I handed them to Daddy, crawled into the back of the truck, and hid under a dirty oil tarp surrounded by empty bowls, buckets, and small washtubs.

The truck rolled onto the toll bridge, and the tires rumbled against the metal grating, causing the floorboard to vibrate. My whole body tingled, but I sat still. I looked at the blackened floorboards and thought about how hard The Blue Goose worked for us. It carried scrap iron in the spring and hauled apples, blackberries, and plums in the summer. He searched the mountains for walnuts in the fall, and delivered loads of coal not only during the winter but during all the other months as well. He was a truck for all seasons. After a minute or so, the vibration eased. We were on smooth road again.

"Okay," Daddy said. "We're on the other side."

I climbed out from beneath the tarp and sucked in a deep breath of fresh air. Fog rolled and drifted along the riverbanks hugging the road and settled into the broad, grassy bottomlands. We snaked our way along the narrow stretch of pavement and turned left onto a dirt road.

"Now that we're away from the river, the fog won't be so bad," Daddy said. "Won't be too much longer." He pointed to a ray of sun piercing through the treetops.

Soon the sun beamed down on us with all its strength. The hot, humid July day seemed perfect for picking the blackberries our family needed to sell—a small and temporary source of income. I took Mommy's neatly printed store list from my pocket and read over the items: flour, milk, potatoes, beans, sugar, cornmeal—the list went on and on. Daddy and I would have to do an awful lot of berry picking. I wondered if any of my classmates were berry picking, too. And I wondered why I hadn't seen any of them gather scrap iron with their Daddys.

"All right," Daddy said. "Watch out for old farmhouses and barns. Berries usually grow near them."

I put the list away. "What about over there?" I pointed to an old house with a slanted roof.

Daddy's piercing gaze followed the direction of my finger. "No. There's people still living there. You can't pick berries in somebody's yard." He patted my knee. "Keep watching."

I watched and fidgeted at the same time. I sweltered beneath my double-layered clothing: two pairs of pants, two long-sleeved shirts, two pairs of socks, and black arctic boots—all necessary to protect me from briars, insects, sunburn, and snakes. I tucked my hair under an old baseball hat so the briars and thorns wouldn't pull at it.

Soon we neared an abandoned coal tipple. Daddy pulled off the road.

"Let's look here," he said, opening the door. "Berries like to grow in places like this." He grabbed his peg leg from behind the seat and strapped it on. I got out on the other side.

Daddy swung open the doors at the back of the truck, and I crawled inside and gathered the bowls and buckets and stacked them near the edge of the truck.

"Don't forget the oil," he said. "And your stick."

I took the ten-cent bottle of cinnamon oil from the glove box and splashed a few drops around the bottom of my pants, where I'd taped the hem tightly against my legs to keep out insects.

"If you wear a few drops of that on your boots," he said, "snakes won't even come near. The smell must bother their eyes or something. I reckon they don't like that."

I nodded, imagining how awful it must be for your eyes to itch or burn if you didn't have hands to rub them.

"Be sure to beat the ground a few times with your stick before walking up on those berries, now," he reminded me. "That'll scare the snakes, for sure."

I walked carefully through the tall weeds toward the old tipple, making sure I kept clear of the broken fence. Pink and white rambling roses ran wild along both sides, and I didn't want to get tangled in their thorny stems.

Daddy stood near the path where I entered the abandoned site. "Remember now," he called, "only pick the black ones, not the red. Leave the red ones to ripen for someone else."

"Don't worry, Daddy," I yelled back. "I won't pick any red ones." The patch wasn't very big, but the berries were dark and sun-warmed, and soon their juices stained my fingers. I wanted so much to taste one, but since the patch was small, I didn't want to waste even one. We needed the money worse than I needed a berry. Soon I'd checked every thorny branch, but all I got was a little over a quart. I hung my head and studied the ground for snakes as I headed back to the truck.

Daddy and I drove on—I worked my sticks over the rough patches of road—until we came to a caved-in railroad tunnel. New tracks lay across the road, so the old tunnel was no longer needed.

"Let's try here," Daddy said.

I stared at the overgrown meadow and swallowed hard. The weeds looked thick and nearly as tall as me. I wondered if something were hiding in there. I climbed down from the truck, faced the meadow, and took a deep breath. Before I ever stepped a foot into the weeds, I swatted at them with my stick and beat the stick on the ground. I watched, and I listened. I looked all around me, parted the weeds with the stick, and held them back so I could walk through. Strong, tough briars, I knew from experience, could tear through even two pairs of pants. After a few minutes, I felt like the meadow had swallowed me alive, so I looked up and over the weeds to get my bearings. Towering above me hung a beautiful patch of berries on top of the hill above the tunnel.

"There's some," I yelled back to Daddy. "Way up there. See? On top of the tunnel."

"Go on," he said. "Climb up on the left. There's a path, and it looks better on that side." I trusted him, knowing he could see better from where he stood than I could from the thicket of weeds.

When I reached the path, I realized it went straight up the hillside. I took two steps and slid right back down to where I'd started. I tied my bucket to my belt, so I could use both hands to climb. Thick green bushes and small trees had overgrown the path, and long briar branches reached for me like tentacles sprouting from an upside-down octopus. The briars pierced through my clothes and pricked and stung my arms and legs. They caught on my pants and shoes, and I kicked against them even as they scratched me, clawed at me, tried to hold me back. "Quit it!" I said, as if they could hear me. "You can't hold me back, stupid briars. Nothing is going to hold me back."

I climbed onward, stumbling from time to time over yellow, muddy rocks that had washed down from the mountain above. When I finally reached the top, I felt hot, sticky, and sweaty. I tugged at my shirts and pants to let in some air, but I knew better than to take them off.

The berries on the mountainside were bigger and plumper, and I quickly picked about two quarts. This time, I didn't resist; I popped a fat, juicy berry into each cheek, and when I'd devoured them, I did it again. I'd earned those sweet treats. To make sure I didn't spill any of the berries, I took an easier path back down the hillside I discovered when I'd gotten to the top. I'd worked too hard to get those berries to risk losing them down a steep climb.

Back at the truck, Daddy and I dumped the berries into a large, flat pan in the backend. Daddy stored berries in flat pans until time to sell them at the end of the day. This way, they were never mashed, but remained plump and juicy right up until the time you sold them.

The sun became hotter as we passed a few more blackberry patches, but we didn't stop. Other berry pickers had picked the vines clean and stomped them to make a path back to the open road. Daddy told me to leave the patch as best I could, so berries would grow back for other people.

Daddy turned down another dirt road—this one so narrow there was barely enough room for The Blue Goose to pass. Low-jutting limbs poked through the windows, forcing us to lean back in our seats. Always, it seemed, something reached its hands out for us.

Soon the roadway opened up to a shallow, little creek. Tire tracks led down into the creek, but there weren't any on the other side.

"That's funny," I said. "How can there be tire tracks on this side of the creek, but nothing on the other side?"

"Because they didn't go through the creek," Daddy said, pointing to where the tracks curved alongside the creek bank. "Looks like they turned around right here and went back."

Daddy drove slowly through the quiet stream. I poked my head out the window and watched the tires pull through the water. Small stones turned over, and little crawdads buried themselves in the sand.

After we rounded the next curve, on a short straight stretch of road, Daddy slowed the truck. He carefully studied the area. "If I remember right, there used to be an old chicken farm down over this hill. Lots of berries, too." He pulled over and turned to me. "Climb onto the hood and look over there. Tell me if you see anything." He turned off the motor.

I kicked open the door and climbed up the front bumper onto the hood. I couldn't see over the tall weeds and clump of trees. I pulled myself onto the roof of the truck and peered below into a large overgrown meadow. "I see an old rundown house, some fence posts with old rusty chicken wire . . . some bushes, trees, and . . . oh, wow! Lots of blackberries!"

I scrambled down from the truck, grabbed my bucket and stick, and pushed my way through the weeds. I picked berries, stopping now and then to suck a droplet of blood from my pricked fingers, and stopping again to munch on a warm berry and swipe the sweat from my forehead. In no time, the berries had stained my hands—and probably my face as well—a deep shade of violet.

When the overhead sun signaled lunchtime, I stopped to eat a can of Armour Potted Meat, followed by a few sips of water from the Mason jar I'd tucked into my sack. I blew on a handful of berries to clean them and popped them into my mouth. Afterward, I hit the berry field again.

By late afternoon, we had every bowl, bucket, and pan filled to the top. Our berry picking was finished, but our day was far from over. Next, we would sell the berries, and we'd shop at the A & P Supermarket. I removed the tape that gathered my clothes snugly against my wrists and ankles, and I took off one of my shirts and a pair of pants. For the first time since I woke up that morning, I felt like I could breathe. I leaned back in the seat and looked over Mommy's grocery list once more. I smiled, knowing that if we could afford everything on the list, she would be pleased.

Soon we came to the road leading toward the toll bridge. As we inched our way toward the booth, I gave Daddy the last dime and nickel, climbed in the back and sat beside the berries. When I felt the tires vibrate on the metal grating, I sucked in the last, long deep breath I could take for a while, and I covered myself with the tarp.

Later that evening we sold the berries at a nearby coal camp and shopped at the A&P for Mommy's groceries. We weren't able to get everything on the list, but I remembered to make sure we got flour.

Mommy

Dear God,

We didn't get everything that Mommy wanted from the grocery store, and I think she is sad. She hasn't been talking to Daddy much lately. But Daddy and I did the best we could.

Why does she keep singing songs about being lonesome? She's learning a new one about being lonesome and crying. What's she got to cry about? Things are a little better here than when we were on Paint Creek.

God, today when I asked her to teach me how to play the guitar, she got upset with me when I changed the guitar to the other side of my lap. She took the guitar away and said I could never learn to play because I use the wrong hand—I'm left handed.

I'm hurt. What else won't I be able to do because I use the wrong hand?

Kathy

The Best of 1960

Near the end of August, things improved for our family. My parents ordered several Kennedy ink pens, and I sold them for fifty cents each from a cigar box while Daddy begged in front of the dime store. I stood a little ways below him, opened the lid, and let people look inside. They loved the pens immediately, and I sold out fast. I liked selling the pens better than begging with Daddy. Maybe it was because I wasn't tied to one place.

Most people had the correct change, but if they didn't, they bought extra pens to make up the difference. Daddy and Mommy were pleased that they were hot sellers. "When Kennedy wins in November, we'll order more," Mommy said.

All the time I kept thinking about the Welfare and what would happen if we got cut off again. We were extra cautious. Daddy told us to never tell anybody our real names or where we lived while we begged door-to-door or sold items on the street. When people questioned him on the street or at the junkyard, he told them he was Sam Smith from Chauncey, or Clyde Conley from Twelve Pole. He was determined not to lose our Welfare check again. If anyone asked me, I was Nancy or Betty.

The extra money from the pen sales enabled us to buy what we needed for the house. Something always needed repaired or replaced: rotted boards in the living room floor, a ceiling leak, and a new commode tank were only a few things on the list.

I came home on the first day of school in September with my second grade book list. Daddy and Mommy were unloading a supply of commodities from the church. I handed the list to him when they finished. He looked it over. "It's a good thing these groceries came today. We'll need extra money this month for Kathy's books."

I was happy he didn't hesitate to say they'd buy my books and that things were getting better. There was even a good surprise for me. A few days later, Daddy came home with a few cans of paint with only a little in each can. He found them in the garbage out back of a building supply store. "Looks like the company painted a house or something and threw away the leftovers."

The drippings on the sides of the cans revealed the colors on the inside: blue, white, black, and green. I was excited as Daddy pried open the lids. "Get Big Ben," he said.

That evening Daddy and I painted Big Ben's suit blue, his shirt white, and his clock wheel black. He looked so much better. I left his face alone, but somehow I saw him with a red tie. I could wait for red paint. After he dried, I sat him in the living room on top of Mommy's Philco radio.

November came and John F. Kennedy won the election for President of the United States. Daddy completed another order for Kennedy pens, desk sets, and ivory crosses with gold Jesus' nailed at the top and bottom. These sold fast, and after my parents paid for the order, they had a little extra money left over.

I finally got an extra quarter from Daddy and bought a cafeteria lunch at school. As I had imagined, the meatloaf, mashed potatoes, and carrots and peas tasted delicious. I took my time and made each bite last. And, as I ate, I hoped that Daddy might not have to beg during the month of December.

Christmas came. My second grade teacher, Mrs. Maynard, gave our class a party, and I drew names and exchanged gifts with a classmate. And when the teacher opened her gifts, mine sat in the pile with the other students. I will never forget what Mrs. Maynard said that day as she opened my gift. "Kathy, this is the most precious desk set I have ever seen. The white and gold pen resting on the pearly top is beautiful.

I will keep it on my desk all year." I felt proud knowing that I gave her something that she really liked and could use.

She lifted the ink pen out of the holder and scribbled with it. It wrote blue. I knew because Daddy had me scribble with all the pens to remove the wax balls on the end before we sold them on the street. He said customers believed pens were dried out if they picked up one that didn't write the first time. I made sure the wax balls were off all my pens.

Mommy put up a small tree that year, a real one Daddy cut somewhere out of the woods. She strung one set of colored lights and a pack of icicles. It was beautiful standing in the living room in front of the window. And it had a present underneath for Margaret, Noah, and me.

I was glad the best part of 1960 had come at last.

Relatives

"Hand me the half-inch, open-end wrench," Daddy said, his muffled voice coming from beneath The Goose.

I squatted by the front tire and dug through the tool bag. "Here." I stretched at an awkward angle and handed him a wrench.

"Not the right one." He handed it back. "Need a bigger one."

I dug through the bag and handed him a larger one.

That one worked. Daddy changed the oil and completed a few other maintenance checks. We were going visiting, and he wanted to make sure the truck would take us and bring us back. Daddy and Mommy's people were scattered all over Eastern Kentucky and Southern West Virginia. I didn't know which way we were going or where we'd end up.

After Daddy finished working on The Goose, he put his tools away and went in the house to change clothes. Mommy took us to the truck, and we waited for Daddy. Margaret and I sat behind Mommy and Daddy's seats on a long board, same as every trip. Mommy held Noah on her lap. He was nearly three and a half and could sit with Margaret and me, but Mommy let him sit with her. Daddy stepped onto the porch and closed the front door.

"Is the back door locked?" Daddy asked. He held a padlock in his hand.

"Yes, I locked it myself," Mommy answered.

Daddy slid the lock through the hinge and snapped it shut. He continued his questions at the top of the porch steps.

"What about the windows? Did anybody shut the windows?"

"I did," I said. "I shut 'em real tight."

"What about the stove? Is the kitchen stove turned off?"

"Yes, I turned it off," Mommy said. "John, if we don't get started now, we won't get there in time for supper."

It was the summer of 1962, and it had been a long time since we'd visited any relatives. I was ten, and Margaret was five and a half. It was hard to get away from berry picking, coal gathering, and scrap-iron collecting, to go visiting. We lost track of time between visits. When it came to discussing relatives, Mommy and Daddy always said that somehow folks got too scattered in our family, and with no telephones, they were harder to find.

The Blue Goose took the first mountain without much effort. It purred along nicely without any coaxing from Daddy. Usually when it acted up and smoked and choked under the hood, Daddy talked to it, which often calmed it down. Today the truck handled beautifully, thanks to new spark-plugs and an oil change.

Mommy hated spark-plug day. She had fussed at Daddy all afternoon a few days before until those small black and white pieces left her kitchen. Daddy sat at the kitchen table and cleaned them in a pan of gasoline. On snowy days, after he cleaned the carburetor, he would put it in the oven to dry. This helped him put the truck back together quicker. Mommy fumed, right along with the oven. But thankfully it was warm this time, so he let the carburetor dry on the front porch.

The two front side windows, The Goose's only windows, were rolled down, but it was still hot in the backend. Mommy slanted a piece of cardboard out the window and sent the humid August air back to us. The extra wind felt good. Mommy brushed our hair into tight ponytails to keep it from slapping our faces, but it didn't help much. Loose strands wiggled free and beat our cheeks and eyes.

The first mountain, a short one, stood behind us, and we relaxed a little. Whenever we crossed mountains, those of us who rode in the back held onto boards nailed to the sides so we didn't fall off our seats. There was no time for talking, playing games, or arguing when riding in The Goose. You had to pay attention. We watched the dips and turns in the road so we'd know which way to lean. Short straight stretches, curves, and mountains kept us busy.

I liked going places in The Goose. No matter if it was Daddy and me or the whole family, we had an adventure. Daddy pointed out interesting things, like the Jesus statue carved on the tree. One time, we drove up a long, steep mountain and came across an unusually sharp S-shaped curve. Three giant trees stood near the road in the middle of the curve.

"Kathy, I bet I can pass these trees three times," Daddy said. "Start counting."

We entered the bottom of the curve and passed by the trees.

"That's one," I said.

The Goose pulled harder on the steeper, middle part of the curve. We passed the trees again.

"That's two."

The Goose crept along, slower now.

"Come on, Goose. You can do it," I said. "One more." I held my breath as The Goose puttered up the mountain. We passed the third time. "Three!" we shouted in unison.

Daddy pulled over when we reached the top of the mountain. He looked under the hood. "The engine's hot. It needs to cool down. That mountain was a hard pull."

"Let's get out and stretch our legs," Mommy said.

My sister and I walked around for a few minutes, but we stayed near the truck. We looked over the edge of the mountain and spotted a large patch of yellow daisies. We wanted to pick a few for Mommy, but they grew on a ledge and we couldn't reach them.

Minutes later, Daddy checked the engine again and closed the hood. "It's cooled down," he said. "Let's go." Daddy started the truck and pulled onto the road. After the first curve, he switched off the motor. We coasted down the other side to save gas. When the road flattened out, he started the motor. The Goose rolled along as if he had never met that mountain.

After traveling a while, Daddy slowed down.

"Are we there?" I asked.

"No. There's a hearse coming," Daddy said. "We'll show respect for the family." He stopped the truck, and we all solemnly watched as a long black hearse passed by. About twenty cars, headlights beaming, followed it. After the last one passed, Daddy started the motor, and we continued onward. Daddy and Mommy helped each other remember the way. It had been a long time since we had gone visiting.

Daddy slowed down again. "I think their house is somewhere near here."

"Yeah," Mommy said. "Sorta looks familiar."

"Wasn't it a small house that sat across the creek, on the right?" Daddy asked.

I leaned over Mommy's shoulder, and my sister leaned over Daddy's, and we looked out the windows. So many houses sat on the right and more stood across the creek.

"Yeah. And didn't the house run sideways with the creek? And the front porch was kinda boxed in, wasn't it?" Mommy asked.

"There it is." Daddy nodded to a rough lumber house on the other side of the creek. He pulled off the road and parked near the water.

"It sure does look like it," Mommy said. "And I bet those kids playing in the creek are theirs. I forget their names." The three kids, a tall boy, a medium-sized girl, and a smaller girl quit playing and looked up at us.

"Is Polly Ann home?" Mommy asked.

"No, but Georgia is," the tall boy said.

"Well, run tell her that her cousins John and Rosie are here to see her," Daddy answered. All three kids ran. "That must be her sister," Daddy said.

Within seconds, a large woman with black, curly hair stepped out on the front porch. She smiled and waved us in. We walked through the ankle-deep creek as the kids ran back down to join us. They were excited to have cousins visit, and we quickly exchanged names. My sister was happy to have someone her age to play with.

We talked so much you couldn't tell who was talking to whom, with lots of hugs, howdy-dos, and handshakes passing between us. There were lots and lots of smiles.

This is great, I thought. They still like us, even though we haven't visited all these years. Everyone agreed we all had grown and changed so much. How long had it been? No one could remember.

There were the usual questions, of course. I guess people can't remember everything. For instance, Georgia wanted to know all about Daddy's leg and how he lost it. He reminded her that his parents died when he was four and lived with several relatives until he was sixteen. One day he tried hopping a train to look for work in another town and he fell under the train. She acted like that was the first time she had heard that.

Daddy asked her husband, Henry, if he still sold produce from that big garden of his. Henry reminded Daddy that he never sold the produce, only raised enough for the family. There was talk, and talk, and more talk. So much to catch up on after all these years! Finally, the guitars came out, and everyone sat down and sang a few songs while the pinto beans cooked on the stove.

When Mommy asked for the guitar, Henry and Georgia acted surprised. They had forgotten that she was one of the best guitar pickers around, but they were happy to have her sing. Mommy chose Loretta Lynn songs. Everyone clapped, while the kids danced. Mommy clearly was happy to have an audience.

Daddy reached for the guitar, laid it in his lap and slid his two-inch Sears socket across the strings to play "The Wreck of Old Ninety-Seven." He made the strings cry when it came to the part where the train wrecked. There was hardly a dry eye when he sang the part about the way the steam scalded the driver to death. Everyone marveled about his guitar playing, since he only had part of a hand. Soon supper time came.

Georgia turned off the beans to let them cool. No one could eat boiling beans on such a hot day. "It's best to take the boil out," Mommy said, and Georgia agreed. After a while, Georgia called the kids to the kitchen. She told us to find a bowl or something to put our beans in. She ladled beans for each of the kids and placed a small square of cornbread in the center of each bowl.

"Y'all find a place to eat," she said. "The kitchen chairs are for the adults." The younger kids left the kitchen and went outside to eat on the front porch.

By the time my turn came, all the bowls were gone. Georgia looked around the kitchen for something to use. She removed the metal lid from the lard bucket and wiped it with her apron. She filled it with beans, placed a piece of cornbread in the center, and handed it to me. I carefully balanced the lid of beans and walked to the front porch. The kids had taken all the chairs, and there was no room for me. My eyes searched the yard for a chair, but there weren't any. I walked around to the side of the house and found a small boxed-in porch. It held a Maytag washer, several piles of dirty clothes, and an upside down washtub. I sat down on the tub and balanced the lid on my knees.

I had taken only a couple bites of beans when I heard a guitar strum. It wasn't from the inside of the house, because it had been put away before supper. This strumming came from outside the house, nearby. The guitar strummed again, and a young male voice softly began singing a song I'd heard on the radio, "Mrs. Brown, You've Got a Lovely Daughter." I leaned out from the porch and looked around. No one in the yard or on any of the porches next to the house.

The boy continued to sing the first verse. I looked again, and this time, I saw him. A teenager, about thirteen, with long brown hair, perched about seven feet off the ground among the branches of a large white oak. He leaned against the tree trunk and his bare legs and feet dangled from a limb. Cradling a brown guitar in his lap, he was adorable, I thought. He continued the song and stared down at me.

My face grew hot, and I eased back under the porch, out of view. I didn't want him to see me eating beans out of a lard lid. I ate quickly and slipped around the side of the house to the front. I put my lard lid in the sink with the other dishes in the kitchen.

Near dark, lightning bugs flashed, and we chased them through the creek, up in the yard, and around the back. My cousins and I removed the flashing green ends from the insects and placed them on our hands and wrists, making glowing bracelets and rings. We put several lightning bugs in an empty pickle jar and pretended it was a lantern.

The adults talked more after supper and enjoyed their evening smokes. Soon it was time to go. We loaded into the back of the truck and waved to our cousins who stood on the porch and waved back.

"Y'all come back!" they yelled from the porch.

"Y'all come and see us, now that you know where we live," Mommy called.

"We will!" they answered.

Daddy started the motor, turned on the lights, and turned the truck toward home. Mommy and Daddy rolled the windows halfway up to block the chilly night air. They talked in soft voices, recalling the day's events one by one. They talked about how the cousins had changed. Some were bigger, though some seemed smaller than they recalled. They talked about hair color, and who inherited whose looks. They seemed pleased with their people.

Tired and sleepy, my sister and I held on tight as The Blue Goose poked through the darkness and carried us home. The talking from the front seats slowed a little as a vanilla moon appeared and followed us all the way to our house.

Soon Daddy pulled into our yard. He turned to Mommy. "You sure have some nice cousins, Rosie."

Mommy stared at him, her eyes large in the moonlight. "They're not my cousins. I thought they were yours."

Saturday Morning Line-up

I had enjoyed our trip the day before in The Goose, and we didn't get in bed until late. I looked forward to sleeping later the next morning.

I awoke to a spoon tinkling in a glass. It was 6:00 a.m.

"Get in here," Daddy said. "It's medicine time."

I groaned and stumbled out of bed, feeling helpless. There was no talking Daddy out of this. My sister and I had tried for years to convince him we did not need it. But it was no use. His mind was made up. The spoon in the glass told me it was going to be bad. Noah was included this time.

"Line up," he said. "Short ones first. Tall ones last."

We lined up, half-asleep, at the kitchen table where he sat. We fidgeted, dreading what was going to happen. I scanned the tabletop to see Daddy's choice of the day. There it stood. Near the assortment of Mason and jelly jars was a big blue bottle of Phillip's Milk of Magnesia, already opened. We all saw it at once and groaned in unison. Stomach cramps were not far away.

Daddy said nothing, but poured the white, chalky liquid into each of the glasses. He eyeballed each one, measuring the dose. Noah got a very small amount.

Though milk of magnesia was Daddy's choice today, a few times he dosed us with Sal Hepatica, a mineral-salt laxative powder he mixed with water. Other times, he gave us chilled bottles of Citrate Magnesia, a syrup mixed with water. All these remedies made us miserable and sent us to the bathroom about twenty-five times each. The best of the worst for us—if there were such a thing—was Ex-Lax, because these small blocks of chocolate tasted better than the other treatments and caused no discomfort. Not a lot, anyway. We still raced for the bathroom.

The tinkling of spoon against glass finally stopped. The mixtures were ready. Daddy handed each of us a glass. "Drink up," he said. "The faster you drink it, the better. Drink an extra glass of water to wash it down." He pointed to the filled water glasses he'd placed on the table.

"I don't like it," my sister said. "It tastes awful. I'm going to throw up."

"It'll do you good," Daddy answered. "It'll clean you out and get rid of germs. That way, you won't be getting sick."

Noah took a sip and made a face. My sister gagged. My stomach started to clench, and I hadn't even tasted it yet.

"Don't look at each other," Daddy said.

We turned away from each other.

"Drink it down fast, and you can get back in bed." He put Noah on his lap. "You'll be able to sleep a little before it starts working."

I swallowed half before the gagging started. The silky texture instantly turned dry, and it tasted awful. Several minutes passed. Noah finished and Daddy told him to get back in bed. Margaret and I drank the last drops from our glasses. The first part of our suffering over, we gratefully gulped down the water to wash away the nastiness on our tongues and hurried back to bed.

About an hour later, the second part of our misery began. I woke first and scrambled out of bed, racing to the only bathroom in the house. For the rest of the day, night, and the next morning, we stayed in the house and waited for our turn in the bathroom. Even the front yard was too far to visit.

I wondered when I would grow out of this home remedy. Even more, I wondered if any of my classmates drank this stuff. But I wasn't about to ask them.

Bubble Gum Man

I washed dishes while my parents sat at the kitchen table and discussed the bills. A light breeze blew through the screen door and rattled the plastic curtains hanging in the kitchen. It was the summer of 1964, and Daddy still begged on the street, sold scrap iron, and picked berries to earn money for our family.

Sometimes Mommy ironed huge baskets of clothes for miners' families. It took every penny we had to pay rent and utilities, buy groceries and schoolbooks for Margaret and me. The rusted Goose barely held together. Daddy used Bondo putty on the fenders and doors. The Goose had failed inspection and Daddy couldn't get a sticker until he removed the rust. And that meant more money that we didn't have.

The clinking of barrels in the back alley alerted me. The Bubble Gum Man, who lived a mile down the road, always came on Tuesday. I dried my hands and followed Margaret and Noah out the door. The beaten, black Ford drove slowly through the dirt alley and parked midway between the two rows of houses.

Rough lumber framed the truck's sides and supported the dented, rusted barrels. Slop from inside the barrels sloshed and spilled as he drove through the alleys. Screen doors opened and slammed shut and kids bounced off porches and ran to meet him. The Bubble Gum Man got out of the truck and walked to the backend. He had gray hair and a wrinkled, tanned face. Years of carrying heavily loaded buckets had slowed his stride and bent his shoulders.

Kids pushed and shoved to be first in line. He ignored them and removed two five-gallon buckets and went about his work of collecting food scraps for his hungry pigs. He entered back yards and emptied the pots that hung on back porches, fence posts, and clothesline hooks—the food scraps that people saved for him. He was careful not to spill any of the slop on the ground. Only squeaky back gates announced his coming and going; he worked silently, not talking to us kids.

He returned to the truck with his buckets, dumped them into the sour-smelling barrels, and closed the tailgate. He plodded to the front of the truck and removed a small brown bag from under the seat.

"Line up," he said.

The children ignored him and kept pushing, shoving, and squealing. Without speaking, he opened the small, crumpled bag and slowly distributed pieces of gum, one by one. It was like Christmas for us when we peeled open the pink, square packages of Bazooka.

For coal-camp children, bubble gum was not an everyday occurrence. I made my piece last all week. I chewed it a little each day and hid it in an empty egg hole in the refrigerator, making it last until the next Tuesday.

I, too, stood in line, anxiously waiting bubble gum. I lifted the younger ones up to him, helped them unwrap the pieces, and read the funnies to them written inside the wrapper. Quickly, they popped the gum into their mouths and disappeared down the alley. Margaret and Noah, too.

But on this day, as I stood last in line, he mumbled, "Ain't you too old for bubble gum?"

I lowered my outstretched hand. We stared at each other for seconds; it felt like hours. Reluctantly, he placed a piece of gum into my hands and continued to stare. I turned away, trying not to cry because of his cutting words. He tossed the half-empty bag on the seat and started the motor. The truck disappeared around the curve, taking the foul odor from the barrels with it.

I trudged up the alley, pausing in front of our house, and pushed on the old gate with both hands. Somehow, it seemed harder to open than before. The heavy cinderblock counterweight had always let me enter without much effort. This time, it stuck. I gathered my strength, forced it open, and quickly stepped inside the yard, where I lingered for a long time. I pondered his last words—*too old for bubble gum.*

I was not welcome at the bubble-gum man's truck anymore. I was only twelve. There had to be a way for me to get my own gum. That night, I went to bed and thought for a long time. I came up with a plan.

The very next day, I walked the railroad tracks, looking for pop bottles. In fact, I began making that walk daily. Mr. Thompson at the old company store gave me three cents for each bottle. When I had enough, I traded those coins for bubble gum. I would never be too old for bubble gum.

Survivor

"Run, you little devils!" Mommy yelled as she lit the four burners. "I'll getcha before the day's over!" Roaches darted from under the burners and scattered across the top of the stove. She blew out the match, turned the knobs on *high*, and smacked them with a rolled-up newspaper.

The roaches we'd killed on the first night in our *new* house had friends, and over the course of the next six years, those friends moved in. Each month, Daddy bought roach spray and Mommy sprayed the house down. Now, six years later, the daily bug battles continued.

This was the day we were going to get rid of them for good. Almost everything in the house had been carried outside waiting to be sprayed. And every inch inside the house would be sprayed and cleaned, as well. This was the last day we were tolerating those pests.

I placed the box I'd filled on the kitchen table. "Where do you want this?" I asked. "It's the last one."

Mommy whacked a roach as it ran across the stove. "What's in it?" she asked.

I peeked inside. "Mostly stuff from the bedroom cabinet; hair rollers, envelopes, song books, and my new Kodak camera." I lifted the camera from the box. I'd sold pop bottles and washed a lot of dishes for a neighbor to earn enough money to buy the camera, and it was my prized possession. Sometimes the neighbor gave me twenty-five cents, and other times, I received a hand-me-down dress or a pair of shoes as payment. I never knew what I would get. Although I needed the money,

I was happy to receive clothing, too.

Mommy stopped swatting and flipped through a couple of songbooks I'd tucked into the box. I snuck a peak at my beautiful new black and gold camera. I'd bought it the week before and couldn't wait to take pictures of my friends and me.

"Put it in the yard, but separate it from the other boxes," she said, placing her favorite mixing bowl on top. "As soon as your Daddy gets back, we'll get started."

It was only mid-morning, but I was already tired. Mommy and I had started early. We took down the curtains and carried out the sheets and blankets. We shook each piece and knocked out hidden roaches. We emptied kitchen drawers and carried out dishes. Our house was nearly bare except for the iron beds and refrigerator. We had fought roaches for years, but we had never emptied the house before.

Mommy killed three more roaches as they ran out of the stove. I glanced out the screen door to make sure the alley was clear. The last thing I wanted was to be seen carrying all these boxes. I imagined what I'd hear from the neighbors. *Hey, what's up with the boxes? Are you guys moving?*

I'd have to come up with an answer, but what? What could I possibly say about stacks of boxes piled along the fence? Even more, how could I explain the clotheslines strung with dry sheets and curtains? I'd never tell anyone we were killing roaches!

Saturdays usually brought everyone in the neighborhood out early to begin their errands. A few of our coal-camp neighbors walked down the alleys between the rows of houses and across the tracks to the post office. Others hurried to the Island Creek Company Store for eggs or bread. Some loaded into their cars and headed to the A & P or Kroger. I paused at the doorway, and when I didn't see anyone, I hurried out the back door and set the box away from the others.

Back inside, I went to my bedroom and sprawled on the naked mattress. I imagined a new room with pink wallpaper and flowered curtains. No more roach antennae wiggling from under the dresser, no more sharp-angled legs running up the bedspread. No more roaches smashed against the inside lip of the refrigerator door. They looked like brown specks of pepper as we scrubbed them off the rubber casing.

Mommy appeared in the doorway and glanced around. "Did you empty everything out of here?"

"Yes. I emptied everything."

"How about under the bed? There's nothing under the bed, is there?"

"No. I checked everywhere."

"Only making sure," she said. "This time, we want to get all of them." She headed for the other bedroom.

I let out a long puff of air. I wanted to be like other girls my age, girls who invited each other over to play records and share popcorn and Kool-Aid. I was sure they weren't embarrassed by roaches crawling in their spoon drawers or on their furniture. How nice it would be to finally invite someone to spend the night, maybe Debbie, who'd recently moved in a house in the back row. We were becoming good friends. Soon, I thought. I could hardly wait.

I ran my hand over the dresser top where I usually kept my books, and I thought about school. This fall, I would not leaf through my books on the back porch looking for roaches. This winter, I would not give my coat ten shakes before putting it on. *Dead.* Once and for all, the roaches would be dead. It was a huge investment in time and money, but we had to do it.

Mommy coaxed my brother and sister out of their sleep and fixed them a quick breakfast of oats. She had them dress quickly and sent them outside to play.

The door opened, and Daddy set a large A & P Supermarket bag on the table. "Surely this will do the job," he said. "I bought a new spray, since that other spray isn't working." He removed four large cans with the words *Roach Killer* emblazoned on the side.

Mommy read aloud from one of the labels. "It says here it will kill roaches on contact and back in their nests. That's exactly what we need." She grabbed a can and went into the living room. "We may as well get started in here. There's less chance of one getting away, if we all work in the same room." Daddy and I each grabbed a can and followed her.

"Let's spray behind the furniture first," she said pointing to our green vinyl couch. "And don't forget to tear off the loose wallpaper and spray the wall real good."

The walls looked bare without Mommy's calendars and Jesus pictures on them. Since we had moved in, her collection had grown from two to twenty-two. I believe she had a picture of Jesus doing everything from holding a baby lamb, walking on the water, knocking on someone's door, to kneeling by a big rock. She also had several from dry cleaners with pictures of little girls wearing ribboned hats and white gloves praying in a chapel and churches with tall white steeples sitting beside large golden maple trees. Sometimes I imagined wearing a hat like hers and going to the same church in the picture. When Daddy told her she had too many calendars on the walls, she'd bring another one home on check day.

Mommy thought it best to remove everything except the larger pieces of furniture. She didn't want to take a chance on roaches hiding inside of anything. "Those little devils are smart and can live anywhere," she often said. "Even underneath my calendars." So we took them down, shook each one, and carried them outside with the other furnishings.

The year before, Daddy decided to kill the roaches with sulfur. Someone had told him that sulfur fumes would definitely kill them, and we would not have any more trouble. Daddy placed several saucers full of sulfur in each room and lit them. Smoke filled the rooms. We waited in the back yard all day, until the sulfur burned out and the smoke disappeared. To passersby, it looked like our house was on fire while we all sat on the grass and enjoyed the scene.

After the smoke had cleared, we went back inside, swept up hundreds of dead roaches, and threw them in the burn barrel. We lived with that rotten egg smell for weeks and kept our doors and windows open all summer.

Before long, though, the roaches came back, and this time, it was worse than before. One night I went to the kitchen, and when I turned on the light, roaches danced everywhere. I had no idea where they'd come from or how they'd arrived in such large numbers, but the roaches had again invaded our house. In fact, it appeared they were holding a welcome-back party in our kitchen. Three or four had even crawled inside the tightly-closed bread bag.

I sighed. I needed to help get rid of these things. Forever.

"Raise the linoleum, and spray under there real good," Mommy ordered. "We can't take a chance on even one surviving."

We went from room to room, pulled back the linoleum rugs, and doused underneath each one. We double-doused the corners of the rooms, where rain-soaked boards had rotted. Even our beds and dresser drawers were not spared from the poisonous spray.

"That should've killed every one of them," Daddy said, turning to Mommy. "There couldn't be a survivor in the place."

By afternoon, the roach battle was over. Mommy and I swept up dust pans full of slick, brown bodies and mopped the floors with bleach. Curtains were hung, beds were made, and dishes, pots, pans, and utensils were washed and placed into freshly scrubbed cabinets and drawers.

"Here's the last one," Mommy said, handing me a small box. "I think it goes in the metal cabinet."

I peered inside: hair rollers, envelopes, song books, and my new Kodak camera. I hurried to the bedroom to unload the few items, so I could watch TV. I placed all the items on the top shelf, with the exception of my camera. I wanted to look at it once more before I put it away.

I removed it from the box and admired the bold black-and-yellow case. Once more, I imagined myself snapping pictures of my friends during my first sleepover. I couldn't wait. I raised the camera to my eyes and pretended to take a picture.

Two waving antennae moved across the small lens. I quickly turned the camera around and checked the front. Nothing was there. Was I imagining things? Did I have roaches on the brain? I raised the camera again to my eyes. Antennae waved from the top left corner, inside the lens.

My heart skipped a beat, and I nearly dropped the camera. I sat motionless on the side of the bed until I gathered enough nerve to look again. Yes, the roach was real. I had seen antennae peeking from inside the corner of the TV too many times to be wrong. First you see the wave, followed by the mad dart across the screen. Antennae appear from nowhere. They rise from the back of the couch, or wave from the sides of curtains. I remembered Mommy's words, "Those little devils are smart and can live anywhere."

I took the camera and Daddy's ball peen hammer to the porch. I placed the camera on the first step, took a deep breath, and smashed it, knocking off the back. I hit again and again, until I came to the lens. I peeked inside and saw the antennae waving at me.

I smashed the lens box, finally exposing the small brown body hiding inside. "No survivors," I said, and I came down hard with the hammer.

Later that evening, Mommy popped a large bowl of popcorn, and everyone settled down to watch TV. I'd placed Daddy's hammer back in the toolbox, thrown my broken camera in the trash, and now joined them in the living room.

"That's what we should have done a long time ago," Mommy said. "Those sulfur bombs didn't even try to kill them. I think it fed them."

"Well, now we know this stuff works," Daddy said. "I'll buy it the next time."

"There won't be a next time." I said, crossing my arms.

"We sure showed them," Mommy said. "I didn't see any in the kitchen tonight. Nothing on the pots or pans. Nothing around the refrigerator. Sometimes, you got to get mean."

I smiled. We had done it. We had won.

I took my place on the sofa and reached for a handful of popcorn. I glanced at the TV, ready to laugh at *The Addams Family*. A funny brown barrette decorated Morticia's hair. It captured my attention—especially when Morticia moved. The "barrette" scampered across the screen in the opposite direction.

6JE6

Later that summer on a warm, humid evening, we sat on the porch and waited. Pesky gnats made their usual appearance. Earlier, Mommy had made a gnat smoke to chase them away. She lit a corner of an oily rag and stomped out the fire. She twirled the rag in her hand, and dark smoke curled across the porch and into the front yard.

"Get it off the porch," Margaret said. "It stinks." The smoke cut down on the gnats, but the hot, humid air and the smoke made it difficult to breathe.

Mommy tossed the rag into the yard and went inside. I couldn't wait any longer. I wanted the day to end. I wanted to go inside and do what we had been waiting to do all week.

The screen door opened. Mommy stepped onto the old wooden porch. "John, fifteen minutes left." She slumped down in the metal glider and repositioned the bobby pins in her thick, black hair.

Daddy glanced at her and took a puff on his cigarette. "Everybody stay put. It's not time yet."

Mommy jerked her head around, let out a heavy sigh, and went back inside. I heard the sound of furniture being dragged across the living room floor.

Noah sat on the steps and slung gravels into the dirt yard. Screen doors opened. Mothers stood on porches, and, with cupped hands, called their children home. I listened to kids tell each other "Good night" and promise "I'll see you tomorrow." No more hide-and-seek or kick-the-can. I liked these games, and so did my brother and sister, but we liked what we were waiting for even better.

"A few more minutes," Daddy said. "Let's be patient. Soon everyone will be inside. We can't take a chance on anyone roaming the alleys or hiding behind houses."

When the alleys cleared and the porches were empty, Daddy gave the go-inside signal. He tossed his unfinished cigarette into the yard. One by one, we followed him and worked quickly to get everything ready for the nine o'clock *Movie of the Week.*

First, Daddy pulled the bag of vacuum tubes from under his bed and laid them on the coffee table. Mommy closed the plastic curtains on the windows in the living room and kitchen. I hated when she did that, because it blocked the cool air from blowing through the window screens. I tried not to think about the heat and concentrate only on what was about to happen. I removed the vase of red and white plastic roses from the top of the TV and pulled off the quilt that had covered it all week.

"Now, I am going to tell you one more time," Daddy began, "don't ever tell anyone about us having a TV. If you do, our welfare check will be cut off again. That's all there is to it. No one on welfare is allowed to have a TV, regardless of where you got it. Do you understand?"

"Yes," we each answered. *Moby Dick* would come on in a few minutes, and I wanted to be ready. I remembered the previews from last week, and I couldn't imagine a fish so big. It looked mean and scary.

Daddy only took the TV out of hiding a few times to watch the news and a few other shows. We watched *Gunsmoke, I Love Lucy,* and *Looney Tunes.* I especially liked *Wagon Train.* I often thought that, when I got older, I would go out West and find the furniture the pioneers threw off the wagons. It seemed like they were always pushing grandfather clocks, wooden trunks, and padded chairs off their wagons, to make it up a mountain or across a river.

I had taken an almost religious vow to keep the TV a secret. Every day, I reminded my brother and sister not to talk about it. When

Daddy had brought the old set home only a few weeks before, we could hardly sit still. He carried it inside after dark, not wanting to draw any attention. He traded with the owner of the salvage shop located at the mouth of Mud Fork. I overheard him tell Mommy that he gave him a motor, two old lawnmowers, and a couple of other things I didn't hear. To our surprise, it worked, as long as you changed the tubes often. Televisions used vacuum tubes to deliver pictures and sounds. The tubes sat on circuit boards and faulty tubes were changed by the owner or a TV repairman.

Before the TV arrived, the only other entertainment we had was outside games with the neighborhood children. I also had a small jump rope and a set of jacks. There was also Daddy's homemade checkerboard. He'd drawn spaces on a piece of cardboard the size of a checkerboard. Mommy cut buttons off shirts from the ragbag to use for checkers. She only cut black and white buttons. If you reached the king row, you simply added the same color button to the square.

Our TV sat catty-cornered in the living room. I pulled it out a little and slid in behind it. I carefully removed the tubes from the black drawstring pouch and spread them out on the floor beside me. The glass vacuum tubes ranged from one inch to six inches in length. That's how I laid them out, from shortest to longest.

We had several tubes I had plucked from the backs of old TV and radio sets we found in the dump and the junkyard. My method always worked. As soon as one tube began to flicker, I wiggled it loose. I checked the number on the side and replaced it with another one.

Daddy placed a kitchen chair in front of the TV and leaned the bathroom mirror up against the back of the chair, so it faced the screen. From behind the TV, I positioned the chair and mirror so I could see the picture, too. Since I was the tube changer, I needed to see the screen. I could tell which tube needed changing—horizontal, vertical, contrast, or sound.

I was used to setting up for TV time. Daddy liked to watch *Big Time Wrestling* on Saturday nights, so several times I was allowed to stay up and change tubes for him. He liked Haystack Calhoun, Dick the Bruiser, and The Sheik. I often nodded off after the first fifteen minutes or so, and he'd wake me to change the tubes.

Everyone sat on the couch or floor in time for the movie to start. The familiar music played. An announcer welcomed everyone to the *Movie of the Week*, and a large lion roared and shook his head above the MGM symbol. "That's a good sign," Daddy said. "Any time you see that lion and hear it roar, it means it will be a good show."

My flashlight and dishtowel were ready. After the lion came the introductions of the main players. Later, the great, white whale appeared. I sat behind the TV and watched the movie's reflection in the mirror.

Frequently, I had to shine the flashlight into the back of the set to check the tubes. All was usually well, but I knew it wouldn't last. Hot tubes meant trouble. Old, worn out tubes gave a few minutes of viewing time. We never dreamed of buying new ones, as they cost around five dollars each—precious dollars we didn't have.

Without warning, the screen began rolling upward. Not a slow, steady roll, but a fast, uncontrollable roll. "Check the vertical," Daddy said.

Margaret and Noah groaned. I searched for the faulty tube. I shone the light on the side and searched for its number. This one was numbered *6LU8*. I found a replacement and wrapped the dishrag around the hot tube. I gently wiggled it free, being careful not to get burned. This one slipped out easily.

Moby Dick was exciting! No one wanted to miss a second of action, so I made the tube changes during commercials. The hot tubes were annoying. The longer we watched the old TV, the more frequently the tubes needed to be changed. I was barely able to keep up. The old tubes couldn't cool off fast enough before I had to use them again. I was getting about two minutes or so on each tube.

Soon, the worst thing that could happen actually happened: the sound went dead. Everyone groaned again. I searched with my flashlight to find the trouble. I located tube 6AU6, which wasn't burning. Luckily, I found a replacement, and the sound came back on.

Captain Ahab declared revenge on the great white whale. He and his crew chased it while we all held our breath and waited to see what was going to happen. Suddenly, without a warning, thick black and white horizontal lines covered the TV screen from top to bottom.

"It's the horizontal tube," Daddy said. "Quick, Kathy, check it."

I shone the flashlight into the back of the TV set. Sure enough, the tube wasn't burning. I hurriedly checked through the tubes. There was no 6JE6! Captain Ahab shouted orders to his men. We heard loud, crashing waves. The sailors screamed. Wavy lines rolled down the screen. I searched once more and found a tube with no number on its side, about the same size as the other one. It had the same number of prongs. I held the two side by side and decided to try it. I inserted it into the socket. Nothing happened. The mirror still reflected wavy lines.

"Hurry! Hurry!" my brother and sister yelled. "Can't you fix it? Can't you make the lines stop?"

I found another tube that I thought might work, and I tried it. No luck. Still wavy lines.

"Well, that's all she wrote," Daddy said. "Turn it off. It's too hot. The whole set is too hot."

Mommy shook her head and glanced at Daddy. "It's a shame we can't have a decent TV like other people." She got up and went to the bedroom.

"Can't we listen to the ending?" my brother asked.

"No," Daddy said. "It'll burn up. You'd never get to watch anything else."

Reluctantly, I gathered the tubes from beneath the TV, behind the curtains, and on my lap. I had scattered tubes anywhere and everywhere, because I couldn't keep up with the number of faulty tubes.

Daddy turned on the kitchen light and opened the back door. The first hint of cool air was refreshing. I spread the quilt over the TV, slid the plastic curtains open, and hung the mirror over the sink in the bathroom before heading out to the front porch. Mommy had gone to bed and Daddy stood at the doorway talking to her in a low voice.

I thought about that movie for the next several weeks. I thought about Captain Ahab and Moby Dick, and how I would never know what happened. Summer nearly over, another school year was about to start. I wondered what seventh grade would be like. Would it be as good as my days at Verdunville Elementary? Maybe my teacher would know what happened to Moby Dick and Captain Ahab.

Bend of the River

Bright sunshine peeked through the curtains and landed on my face. I rubbed my eyes and sniffed the air. Someone was frying chicken. Which of our neighbors fried chicken this early in the morning? I went to the kitchen and saw Mommy turning over chicken legs frying in a black iron skillet. She placed two of them onto a brown paper bag to drain, added two floured pieces to the hot grease and gave them a generous shake of salt and pepper.

"What's going on?" I asked. "Are those ours?"

"Yes, they are. Your Daddy is taking us on a picnic."

We had never been on a picnic before. She stirred a pan of boiling gravy on the back burner and removed a pan of golden brown biscuits from the oven. A large bowl of fried potatoes sat on the side of the stove. I was excited. Maybe this would cheer Mommy up a little. She seemed sad ever since the TV stopped working a few weeks ago.

"Get a pair of shorts for you and the kids and come back and help me pack," she said.

I practically ran through the house and woke Margaret and Noah. "Get up! We're going on a picnic!"

After dressing them in shorts and shirts, I went to the kitchen to help Mommy. We cut empty bread bags in two and placed them over the bowls of potatoes and gravy and covered them with pot lids. Mommy slid the pan of biscuits into a large A & P grocery bag and put the chicken into the pot she used to cook beans.

She set her small dishpan on the table. "Here," she said. "Put five plates and five spoons in here and take it to the front porch. You can help your Daddy load when he gets back. I'm gonna get me a pair of shorts."

Minutes later Daddy pulled in and opened the back doors to The Goose. I handed him the dishpan, and he set it beside Mommy's large washtub in the backend. A large block of ice sat in the middle surrounded by several cans of grape and orange soda. "Wow!" I said. "I can't wait. Where are we going?"

"You'll see," he said. "Bring me the rest of the food. We need to get going so we can find a good spot on the river."

Within a few minutes The Goose was loaded with good food and happy people. We smiled, talked and laughed, anxious to get our picnic started. About an hour later, we turned off the highway onto a dirt road to gain access to the river. The road opened up to the water's edge at a bend in the river. Sand collected on one side of the bank, making a small beach on the right side; a semi-rocky bank lay on the left side. The slow-moving stream, green as the leaves that hung from the trees along the bank, invited us. Mommy's eyes widened. She secured the bobby pins in her hair and pushed open the door. "Let's go!" she said. Lucky for us, there were only two other swimmers there.

"Wait a minute," Daddy said. "I need to get parked."

"Can we get in?" Margaret asked.

"Let's get out now," Noah said. "I want to look for crawdads."

Daddy turned The Goose around and backed near the water on the rocky side. "We'll open the back doors and use the backend as a picnic table," he said. "You kids stay near the bank and don't go near the water until I tell you." We nodded.

Mommy dashed out of the truck and ran toward the slow-moving stream. Daddy opened the back doors and handed us a few empty cans. "You can make sand castles out of these," he said. "And you might find a crawdaddy or waterdog."

We happily took the cans and headed for the sand. Mommy waded into the stream until it came to her chest and began swimming. I had never seen Mommy swim before. She splashed around and told us how good the water felt. She smiled and waved to a couple of teenagers on the bank. They smiled and waved back.

I played in the sand with Margaret and Noah and helped them make a fort with the dumped cans of sand. We used river rocks and wide leaves for flags and roofs. Mommy floated and played in her large green pool of water while Daddy scouted the river from a trail on the upper bank. He looked up and down the river and came back.

He pointed to a fallen tree half in and half out of the water. "See that water birch?" Don't go any further beyond from where it hit the water. It's only a foot deep there. You'll be fine." We nodded. Daddy sat down on the water birch and watched us and Mommy.

The kids and I waded into the water where Daddy said we could go and sat down. We wiggled our feet in the warm water and rinsed the sand from our arms and hands. We filled our cans and took turns pouring water on our heads. I was having fun until Margaret spoke.

"What's on your leg," Margaret asked, pointing to my mole.

"It's a birthmark," I said.

"What's that?"

"Mommy said I was *marked with a hamburger* because she craved one before I was born."

"It's ugly. Why don't you pull it off?"

"Never mind," I said tugging at my shorts. They barely covered the brown circle, and if she thought it was ugly then everyone else would too. I decided to keep it hidden from then on.

A little while later, we followed Daddy to the back of the truck. Mommy saw us and came too.

She stood at the backend and fixed each of us a plate with chicken legs, fried potatoes, gravy, and biscuits. I couldn't wait to taste her crispy fried chicken. No one could out-do her. We often fought over the crisp bits left in the skillet. Daddy gave us a soda pop. We sat on the water birch, laughed and ate.

"Make sure you put your plate and spoon back in the dishpan,"

Mommy said before heading back into the water for another swim. After playing in the sand a little more, Noah spoke up. "Daddy, I'm tired. Can we go home now?"

"I believe so," he said. "It's about time."

Daddy closed the doors to The Goose and we piled in. Mommy came out of the water, dried off a bit, and climbed inside. No one found any water dogs or crawdads, but Margaret and Noah picked up a few shiny river rocks. I didn't find anything at the river, but I enjoyed being with my family and playing in the warm brown sand and calm green water. For one day, there was no picking, gathering, or shoveling—only peace and relaxation at the bend in the river. On that day, it seemed that Mommy was happy too.

A Quarter and a Penny

It was the first day of school, and I was excited to enter junior high. The older teenagers told Debbie and me about the Gold N Blue, a hotdog stand near the school, but all I had was a nickel for milk. I wanted to eat lunch there on my first day, but I wasn't able to earn any extra money before school. My neighbor gave my dish washing job to her older daughter now that she was home. So until I could find work, I would have a sandwich and milk for lunch.

When the bus driver blew her horn, I walked to the bus stop. I wondered what Mommy and Daddy would do during the day, now that all of us were in school: Margaret in the third and Noah in the first. Three sets of books to buy now.

Other kids from the camp joined me at the bus line as the bus came back down the road. We piled on, chatting away, complimenting each other for getting out of summer shorts and tops. Even though I didn't have spending money, I was thankful for one thing. The postmaster gave me two bags of clothes that her daughter no longer wore. Mommy managed to make them fit by hemming and seaming the dresses. I was happy to have a *new* dress to wear.

This was the first time I had ridden a bus to school. Logan Junior High was located in the upper end of town. It took about thirty minutes for the bus driver to pick up all the students on the route and drop us off in front of the school. We had a short assembly, and I followed other students to the seventh grade section of the school and entered Room 7A.

"We have a football game tomorrow," Mrs. Brooks said. "I'm collecting money today." She closed the classroom door.

The tardy bell rang, and Mrs. Brooks plopped her plump self behind her tiny desk in front of the classroom. Those of us who'd come in last scrambled to find a place to sit. I found an empty desk in the back of the third row. I opened my notebook, ready to write.

With a push from her index finger, Mrs. Brooks adjusted her glasses and shuffled the papers on her desk. She was an older teacher, and she'd dressed in red from head to toe; large red earrings, a red-flowered dress, and shiny red heels.

"Those math problems are for you," she said, pointing to the blackboard. On a bulletin board to the left of the math problems, a twelve month calendar highlighted the current month of September, and on top, *1965* was stenciled in large white numbers.

"Get started. There'd better not be any talking." And, as an afterthought, she jabbed a finger toward the window. "The pencil sharpener is over there." A small metal oval with a hand crank was mounted beside the window.

I searched through my purse for a pencil, being careful not to mash my jelly sandwich.

My sixth-grade teacher had told us junior high was a lot different than elementary school. We asked what she meant. She said the teachers were stricter and expected us to be serious and mature at all times. I had been in seventh grade for less than thirty minutes and I knew what truth she had spoken.

I wrote my name on my paper and began working on the multiplication problems. They weren't difficult. I had mastered 4-digit-times-4-digit problems in the fourth grade. I was good at them.

Everyone worked quietly. Mrs. Brooks took roll and fumbled around her desk. She seemed to be looking for something. She must have opened and closed the top and bottom drawers a half-dozen times. Finally, she pulled out a roll of gray tickets and placed them on her desk.

"All right," she began. "I always collect ballgame money early. So I want you to come up a row at a time and buy your ticket. I will mark off your name."

She pointed to the row near the door. "We'll start with this row. Come here and bring me a quarter and a penny. I'll give you a ticket. It's up to you to hold on to it. You're old enough not to be losing things. This is not grade school."

The students in the first row got up and walked to her desk. She collected money from the first two kids, gave them a ticket, and was about to take care of the third one.

"I didn't bring any extra money today," the tall, skinny girl said. "I only brought a quarter for my lunch."

I thought exactly the same thing about me. I didn't bring any extra money, and I surely didn't have a quarter. Daddy laid out five nickels on the table last night—one for each day of school this week. He told me I was old enough to be responsible for my milk money, so I took one nickel, and put the other four in my bedroom cabinet.

"Well," Mrs. Brooks said, "if you have to use today's lunch money, do it. I don't think it will hurt you much. Your supper will taste that much better." The girl gave her the quarter. Mrs. Brooks handed her a ticket.

Mrs. Brooks summoned row two, collected money, and handed out tickets. A student whispered something to her. She sprang from her desk and shouted, "I don't want another one of you to tell me you don't have twenty-six cents!" She came around her desk and loomed closer. "I know that *everyone* has money on the first day of school."

She sat down again and motioned for the third row, my row. Those in front of me got up and went to her desk. I kept working on the assignment. Shortly, the students returned to their seats. A blond-headed boy in front of me whispered to a girl in the fourth row that he used the week's milk money to buy his ticket.

In the middle of her routine, she stood up and asked the class, "Has anyone in here ever brought a fried-egg sandwich from home for lunch? Or how about a mashed-pinto-bean sandwich? On ballgame days, bring a sandwich, and use your quarter to buy a ticket. Fried-egg sandwiches and pinto-bean sandwiches never killed anyone."

She called for the last row and sat down to get ready for the first student, Larry, a boy I knew from grade school. Larry's family struggled. His father had been off work for months due to a coal mining injury. Larry bent down and whispered to her.

"Well, give me the quarter, anyhow," she said. "Milk is five-cents, and five times five is twenty-five. You can drink water. It never killed anybody to drink water with their lunch. Next time, you need to plan ahead." Larry handed her the quarter and returned to his seat. The class was quiet. Heads bent low and pencils worked furiously on lined notebook paper.

Meanwhile, Mrs. Brooks seemed to be confused. She ran the eraser end of the pencil through her tightly curled brown hair and stood up. Slowly, she raised one arm, pointed her finger at the first kid in row one and began to count.

"One, two, three, four, five, six," she said. "Seven, eight, nine...," she continued in row two. She glared at each student as she counted one by one. She sat down and marked names off the roster. She counted us again.

"Something is not right." She looked at us sternly. "There are thirty-three of you, and I have only sold thirty-two tickets." She looked at the list again and stood up.

"We have a problem," she said. "Not everyone paid."

I stopped working the problems and stared at her, not moving a muscle.

"There is one poor old Joe who doesn't have any money. We're going to help 'em out." She removed one of her new red heels and held it in front of her. A red bow with a gold buckle covered the pointy end. She walked over to the first row and stood there. No one moved. No one blinked. All eyes focused on her and that shoe.

"All right." She dangled the shoe in front of the first student. "Let's offer a little charity to this poor old Joe. Reach down deep—real deep," she said. "Let's help this poor old Joe go to the game."

She walked up and down the first aisle and held the shoe in front of each student. "Thank you," she said to one girl. "Even a penny helps." A couple of students dropped in a penny. One gave a nickel.

She stared at the few coins and started again. "I know you have it," she said, starting down the second row. "But I also know you want to hold onto it."

She turned and faced the other rows. "Stop saving popcorn money. You can pop your corn tonight and bring it tomorrow in a brown bag." A few more coins dropped into the shoe. They slid down and clinked on the others.

I lowered my head when she begged down the third row, and when she got halfway down the fourth, she stopped. "I think we have enough," she said. She limped to her desk as students whispered. She dumped the coins on her desk and counted them. She added them to the other pile of money.

She stood up, put on her shoe, and reached for the large roll of gray tickets. "We're okay, now." She tore off a ticket.

She walked to the last seat in the third row, *my seat*. She placed the ticket on my desk.

My face burned as hotly as if the ticket were a torch.

The bell rang to change classes. Everyone gathered their books.

"Wait a minute," she said. "You need to understand something. You're in homeroom Seven-A, Mrs. Brooks' homeroom. *My* homeroom. No one in my homeroom ever reports to study hall on game days. It's a waste of time. I never have and never will supervise a study hall. I always have *and always will* have one-hundred-percent attendance at games."

Her eyes locked with mine, and though my throat wanted to swallow hard, my mouth was much too dry. "Class dismissed."

The next day our school dismissed at 11:30, so students could eat lunch and walk to the football field on Middleburg Island, about a twenty-five minute walk. Debbie and I walked together. The streets were crowded with excited seventh, eighth, and ninth graders. Some students bought fresh glazed donuts and vanilla cupcakes from Nu-Era

Bakery. Several waited in line at the candy counter at the dime store and bought bags of popcorn and roasted nuts. Debbie and I never bought anything on our walk through town.

"I have popcorn money, but I'll wait and buy it at the game," she said. "We can share." She was a great friend, and we could tell each other anything.

Passing by the dime store triggered memories of Daddy and me begging there several years ago. I was saddened to remember those times. But when I looked at the ticket I held in my hand, that sadness turned to anger. I did not like that Mrs. Brooks forced my classmates to buy me a ticket, especially when I learned that students from the other classes were allowed to purchase theirs this morning, the day of the game. It was a mean thing for her to do to her students and me. I would never forget how she made me feel.

But again, I learned something from Mr. Brooks. She taught me to be prepared. The next day I went to the office and asked for a ballgame schedule. That year, I did whatever was necessary to have my quarter and penny ready when she asked for it.

Coal Camp Beatles

Two weeks later, the substitute bus driver accidentally rolled past our evening stop. By the time we got her attention, we were in front of the Island Creek Store, a few hundred feet ahead. She opened the door and let us off. Mrs. Taylor, a clerk at the store, was taping a sign to the store window.

Concert
Upstairs in Boy Scout Hall
Saturday Night 7-9
Admission—10 cents
All Beatle Tunes!
Performed by Randy and Tommy

Only a dime? Unbelievable! I grabbed Debbie as soon as she stepped off the bus. "Look at this." She quickly read the poster, and I tugged her arm. "Do you think you can go?"

Debbie and I did everything together: playing records on her record player, doing homework, and lying in the sun. Daddy always agreed with our plans, if he knew Debbie was going. He liked her and her family.

"Wow!" she said. "This sounds great. We don't even have to get a ride. I'll ask Mommy if I can go."

"She can't say no, Debbie! This is a dream come true. Mommy has been cleaning for a woman up the road, and I'm sure I can get a dime.

I'm sure Daddy will say *yes*, if he knows you're going. Go ask your Mommy and let me know as soon as you can."

I had seen the Beatles on *The Ed Sullivan Show*, and I was in love with them and their music. Actually, I first heard them on our hometown radio stations, WLOG and WVOW. Sometimes the stations didn't come in clearly because the battery on my transistor radio was low. Often I had to reposition the dial, because it kept moving off the station. I had a hard time hearing a complete song.

On Wednesday after school, Debbie came over to study for a science quiz. I fixed Margaret and Noah a peanut butter sandwich and then cleared the table. Daddy said Mommy was working up the road again. About an hour later, Debbie's Mommy called her to supper.

"Have you asked if you can go to Randy and Tommy's concert?"

"Mommy said she didn't care but said I have to ask Daddy."

"What did he say? He did say *yes*, didn't he?"

"I haven't asked him yet. He's gone this evening."

"Debbie, you have to ask him tomorrow. If he says *no*, you'll have a couple of days to ask again."

"Okay. I thought I'd wait until about an hour before it starts before I ask. That way it'll be hard for him to say *no*, especially if I'm already dressed."

Margaret came into the kitchen. She folded her arms and smiled. "If'n I can't go, you can't go."

We looked at her. "What?"

I had to think of something quick. I sure didn't want her tagging along. "You're too little. You're only eight. They won't let you in." I said.

She leaned forward and got in my face. "Then I'm telling Mommy not to give you a dime, and I'm telling Daddy not to let you go!" She smiled big and left the kitchen.

"Don't worry about her." I turned back to Debbie. "Be sure to remind him that it's only across the tracks in the Island Creek Store's meeting hall," I said. "That might help him say *yes*."

I grew more excited every day. Getting up and going to school was no problem for me. I had heard that Randy and Tommy were good on the drums and guitar, and I couldn't wait to hear them play. The two boys lived in our neighborhood, and sometimes they walked past our house on the way to the store. Randy was shorter than Tommy, but both had long brown hair and cute smiles. They were friendly and always spoke to me.

On Thursday after school, I began my chores right away. I helped cook supper, swept the kitchen, and started on my homework. Mommy was home that evening and gave me a dime. I wasn't worried about Margaret's little threat because Daddy already said I could go. I speculated on what song they would play first. Would it be "I Want to Hold Your Hand," or "She Loves You?" It didn't matter. I loved both of them.

Friday came, and I raced off the bus to talk to Debbie. "Did you ask?"

"No, but I'm sure it will be all right. He's been in a good mood all week. I think he'll say *yes*. What're you wearing?"

"There's no air conditioning, so probably shorts and a blouse."

"Okay. I told Mommy I would help her clean this evening. Come over tomorrow about six-thirty, and we'll walk over together."

Saturday morning, I woke up early and helped Mommy fix oats and toast for the family, and I cleaned the rest of the house. I did part of my homework and washed my hair. Later that afternoon, I helped make sandwiches and fried potatoes for supper, and ironed my shorts and blouse. At last, 6:30 came.

I took a dime from my coin sock and walked to Debbie's house. Along the way, I saw other young teens walking across the tracks. The windows were raised in the meeting hall, and I heard the men tuning up. The concert would start. We needed to hurry if we were going to get a good seat.

Debbie came to the door. "I'm not ready. I'll be out in a minute."

Through the doorway, I saw her Daddy. He sat in his favorite chair in the TV room. Debbie and her Mommy stood in front of him. I thought, perhaps, she was asking for a dime to pay for admission. I sat down on the front porch glider and waited. I listened as the band warmed up. Guitar and drums played a tune, but nothing I recognized. In a few seconds, Debbie came out and sat down beside me. She was silent.

"Let's go!" I said jumping up.

"Can't."

"What? Didn't you ask?"

"Yes."

"What'd he say?"

"He said, 'Phooey on Randy and phooey on Tommy.'"

I was dumbfounded. "What does that mean?"

"It means I can't go." Debbie got up, went inside, and shut the door.

I was crushed. I walked back to the house and sat on the front porch. I didn't think for a minute about going without Debbie. It was a teenage thing; you didn't go places by yourself. At 7:00 p.m. the windows to the concert hall closed.

So close, and it only cost a dime.

Radio Land

It was the end of September. Mommy turned the radio on and adjusted the tuning dial on the old floor model radio.

"Good morning out there to all of you good little children in radio land," Reverend Smith said. "Jesus loves you and wants you to be saved." His voice blared through the radio once again as he delivered the same opening speech that he had given for years on radio station WOAY from Oak Hill, West Virginia.

"Everybody quiet! *The Old Time Gospel Hour's* coming on," Mommy said.

Time for another Sunday morning sermon. "I'd like to thank Herbert Luther for his $5.00 love offering and Maggie Sims for her $3.00 last week," the reverend said. "Everyone, please keep those donations coming."

After naming the givers and the amounts given, the reverend read the names on the prayer list. "Listeners, please bow with me now and offer a prayer to the Lord for these souls who stand in need."

Margaret and Noah played quietly in a sand pile in the front alley, one of their favorite spots. I sat on the front porch where I knew Mommy and Daddy would soon settle. The open windows and front door allowed the Philco's voice to flow loud and clear beyond the next alley.

"Friends and neighbors," the reverend said, "our ministry is in trouble. We need financial assistance, and our tabernacle needs wood and coal for the upcoming winter season. We're asking you to dig deep and pray hard during this broadcast. Ask God prayerfully what you can do to help keep our ministry on the air and coming to you on this station's airwaves."

Mommy and Daddy sat in their rusted, painted-to-death, red porch chairs, and I stretched out in the metal glider. "It's a shame that no one will help that poor preacher," Mommy said. "He begs for help every Sunday. You'd think that someone would have done something to help him by now."

"And now, brethren," the reverend said, "let's sit much in prayer as Sister Bessie sings our opening hymn, 'Keep on the Firing Line.'"

Mommy and Daddy drank coffee and listened to Sister Bessie belt out the first verse. This Sunday, like every Sunday, Mommy had risen early, cooked oats, and dabbed at the house. She straightened the flowered cover on the sofa and swept the crumbs from under the kitchen table. And always, by 11:00 a.m., her chores were completed and a second pot of coffee signaled, "Take me off, I'm done."

The hymn played on, and Sister Bessie bellowed the words to verse two.

Margaret stood up from the sand pile with hands cupped over her ears. "Turn it down!" It's too loud, and it's hurting my ears."

"That guitar needs tuned," said Mommy.

"No, she's singing too loud," Daddy said. "That'll make a guitar seem out of tune. Go ahead and turn it down a little."

Mommy loosened the black friction tape from the volume knob. She tightened the tape a bit. The volume had been hard to control ever since Daddy brought the radio home. Several years ago, he'd traded a refrigerator motor for it. The brown Philco, complete with a short-wave band, couldn't bring in the *Old Time Gospel Hour* all by itself, nor the *Grand Ole Opry* on Saturday nights, without Mommy's help. One day, she attached a thin piece of copper wire to the back of the set, ran it across the living room, out the window, and up the side of the house to the roof. She fastened it to an aluminum rod. Neighbors marveled at her makeshift antenna.

Sister Bessie finished the hymn, and Mommy shushed everyone. Reverend Smith was ready to deliver his hellfire-and-brimstone message.

"We are all sinners, saved by the grace of God," the reverend said. He spoke fast and hacked out his message in rapid breaths, hardly stopping at all. He cut it off quickly when the gospel hour was nearly over and it came time to give his address and tell others out there in radio land where to mail their donations.

At the conclusion of the gospel hour, Mommy and Daddy sat and talked for a long time. They moved their discussion into the kitchen so Mommy could put water into the pot of boiling beans.

"Well, Rosie, that settles it," Daddy said. "We can't let that poor preacher down. He has cried 'Help!' long enough. We'll see what we can do."

The next Saturday we all rose early at 8:00 a.m., piled in the old panel truck and headed toward the coal tipple in Kanawha County. Daddy's friend, the loader, was on duty. Daddy talked with him, and we backed out of the way like we used to do. We took turns picking up lumps of coal that had fallen off the trucks and beltline and loaded them into The Blue Goose. Daddy sent me scrambling down over the mountain to get the larger, bucket-sized lumps that had fallen off the trucks. By mid-afternoon, we had a truckload and were ready to go.

Daddy pulled away from the tipple, drove until he reached the hard road, and turned onto another road that I wasn't familiar with. "Rosie, I don't know this area that well. Help me watch for the name of the tabernacle. It's out here somewhere."

"John, the announcer said that you make a left where the road forks. That should put you right at the tabernacle. Reverend Smith is supposed to live out there somewhere near it. I'll watch the best I can, but it's hard with Noah squirming on my lap." Noah was in first grade, but still loved to sit up front with Mommy. Margaret and I rode in our usual spot on the board behind Mommy and Daddy's seat. Now that I was older and bigger, I barely had enough room to sit between their seats and the sheet of plywood that separated us from the mound of coal in the back. I wished we could get a car like everyone else. The Goose, about seventeen years old, broke down nearly every week or so.

"Take a left here," Mommy said pointing. "It shouldn't be too far after this." Daddy obeyed her and continued for a few miles down a curvy road.

Finally, Mommy spied it. "This is it. Turn here onto Parker Avenue."

We drove slowly down a paved street past aluminum-siding houses with white fences that shot up out of the ground straight and tall. Faded gold chrysanthemums lay abundantly along the fences, and scarlet sage scattered across front yards.

"Oooh, look how pretty," Mommy said. "What beautiful houses. Did you see those flowers back there?"

Daddy geared down and The Blue Goose crept along more slowly. "Look for the names on the houses," he said. "See, that one says *B. Taylor*. Be sure to check the houses on both sides of the road."

My sister crammed in behind Daddy's seat. She peered out his window and pointed to a red swing set in one of the yards. I looked, too, taking in all the pretty porch chairs and lacy curtains hanging in the windows.

"There it is," Daddy said. "F. Smith. The *F* must stand for *Franklin*." Daddy pulled off the road and parked in front of the house. "Come on, Rosie. Let's go see if anybody's home. Katherine, you watch the kids."

I climbed into Mommy's seat so I could get a better view. My brother and sister crowded alongside me. We watched Mommy and Daddy walk up the steps to the immaculate, gray-painted porch. They opened the storm door and knocked.

A tall, heavy-set man with black, wavy hair opened the door. Daddy told him something and pointed to the truck. The man, dressed in a clean white shirt and dark slacks, stared at our beat-up truck and at our three dirty faces peering out the front window. He focused on Daddy's peg leg and Mommy's dirty sweater. Slowly, he raised his hand and pointed down the street to a large, white building on the right. Mommy said something to him and reached out and placed two one-dollar bills in his reluctant hand. They shook hands, and Mommy and Daddy came back to the truck.

"Was that him? Was that the man who preaches to us on Sunday?" I asked as they got back into the truck.

"Yes, that is Reverend Smith," Mommy said. "And, boy, was he surprised to see us. Why, I don't think the man said more than four or five words. The way he looked at us you'd think that he'd just seen a ghost."

"He was too thankful to speak," Daddy said, as he pulled up to the tabernacle.

Daddy swung the back doors of the truck as far as they would open and shoveled coal into the Reverend's bin. I climbed on top of the load and pushed the larger lumps down to him. When his shovel stuck deep in the pile, I wiggled it loose. For a long time, I fed Daddy's shovel as he decreased the load on the truck and increased the pile in the coal bin. Daddy's strong arms commanded the shovel to dig deep, throw hard, and pile high. Finally, we'd loaded all the coal into the bin. Daddy threw the shovel into the back of our empty, dirty truck.

"Let's go home," he said. "We're finished."

I stared at Reverend Smith's house as we drove down the street. He stared at us, too, from his front window. He peered through parted curtains and watched us until we reached the end of the street.

The following Sunday, Mommy rose early and followed her usual routine. At eleven o'clock, the family gathered around the Philco once more for the Reverend Franklin Smith's *Old Time Gospel Hour*. Sister Bessie still belted out the opening hymn. Reverend Smith delivered the same hellfire-and-brimstone message.

At the end of the program, Mommy switched off the Philco. She and Daddy went into the kitchen, and I followed.

"How come he didn't say anything about 'You good little children out there in radio land'?" I asked.

No one answered.

"John," Mommy said, filling their cups with coffee, "He never said anything about us bringing him that load of coal, or the two dollars we gave him. Wonder why?"

Daddy picked up his cup and stared at the dark liquid. He blew into the cup a couple of times like I had seen him do before. He looked out the kitchen window before he said, "Maybe he forgot."

I remembered how hard he worked filling the reverend's coal bin. Was Daddy remembering that too? Or was he thinking how difficult it was to buy gas for The Goose to make the trip to the tabernacle or anywhere else?

"Kathy, grab that can of salmon from the cabinet," Mommy said. "In a few minutes you can help me peel potatoes for supper."

I searched in the bottom of our only cabinet—the one with the large red rooster decal on the top left door of the flour bin. I found the salmon easily, because there were only a few cans of food left: one of mustard greens, two tomato soups, one corn, and one pork 'n' beans.

Daddy sat quietly and finished his coffee.

"He could have at least mentioned that one of the listeners delivered him a load of coal for the tabernacle," Mommy said.

"Yes, he could have," Daddy said.

I wondered why Daddy didn't have any comments about the reverend not thanking us like he did other people on all the other Sunday mornings. Was it because Daddy was ashamed of asking people for things, too? But, we always thanked people when they gave us something.

Trick-or-Treat

Margaret Ann pulled back the curtain and looked into the alley. "It's almost dark. They'll be out soon."

Noah jumped off the sofa and joined her. "Yeah, and we can't go. We don't have anything to wear." He sank back on the sofa and continued biting his nails.

The Island Creek Coal Company store across the railroad tracks had plenty of masks to choose from: witches, clowns, monsters, and even a white mask of Casper, the Friendly Ghost. My brother and sister had looked at the masks every day for two weeks now, but there was no money to buy one.

Margaret closed the curtain and cracked the door a little. She poked her head through the opening and peered out. "I think I hear somebody coming up the alley." She eased the door shut and slumped on the sofa beside Noah.

I swept crumbs from beneath the kitchen table as Mommy washed the last pot. Suddenly, she stopped washing and stared at the wall in front of her. She pressed her lips together and inhaled deeply. A second later she let out a sigh, rinsed the pot and put it away.

"Hold on," she said hurrying through the house. Within seconds, she returned to the kitchen and placed a large crumpled bag on the table. She grabbed a knife from the spoon drawer and went into the living room.

"Y'all come in here," she said. "Help scoot this couch away from the wall."

Quickly, we scooted the couch about three feet away from the wall. Mommy placed her hands in the middle of the wall about four feet from the floor and felt around.

"It's got to be right here," she said, marking a spot. She jabbed the knife into the heavily layered wallpaper and cut a straight line about four feet across.

"What are you doing?" I asked.

"Watch," she said. "This room needs new wallpaper anyhow." She cut a line down the wall on both sides of the horizontal cut. She removed the large piece of cardboard that covered the hole and leaned it against the couch. Cool, musty air rushed from the opening.

It was a good thing Daddy had not returned from the junk yard because he would not have liked it. I couldn't believe she actually cut a large hole in the living room wall. I had never seen her do anything like that.

We stared at the old fireplace, blackened with years of soot. This was the first time we had actually seen it. The family before us had sealed all the fireplaces and placed small gas stoves on the hearths. Mommy stuck her hand into the fireplace and brought out a palmful of black soot.

"Come over here," she said, kneeling in front of the hole. "Tonight, we will trick-or-treat as black haints." I opened my mouth, but nothing came out. She rubbed soot on our faces. It felt cool and smelled smoky.

Next, Mommy grabbed the bag from the kitchen table and emptied it onto the floor. She pulled out a large shirt and put it on Margaret. Next, she found one for Noah. Finally, she ripped off two pieces of material and tied the pieces around their heads.

"There." She stepped back and admired the costumes. "You look like little spooky haints! Go into the kitchen and find a paper poke to put your candy in."

She turned to me. "Here," she said, handing me a shirt. "Put this on and find a pair of pants. Run to the kitchen and get us a paper poke. I'll lock all the doors and close the curtains. We'll sneak out the kitchen door and go through the back alley."

A few minutes later, Mommy came back. Her face was black, her hair was tied up, and she wore a shirt and pair of pants she pulled from the bag.

"Are you dressing up, too?" we yelled.

"Let's go," she said opening the door. "Be quiet until we reach the main alley. Part of the fun of dressing up on Halloween is not to let anyone know who you are."

My heart pounded. We were going trick-or-treating. With Mommy!

In a minute or so, we strolled through the alley alongside a beautiful Cinderella, a little red devil, and a one-eyed monster. Coming up behind us were witches, ghosts, and other goblins. It would have been great to have a real costume like they did. Soon the camp was crowded and porches were overflowing with trick-or-treaters.

Mommy led the way as we visited our first house. "Trick-or-treat!" she yelled, opening her poke. A little pirate with a black eye patch and red wax lips stared at us and jumped in front when the door swung open. A large woman held a bowl of suckers as she glanced over our little crowd.

"How cute you are!" she said, putting a sucker into the bags of the little pirate, scarecrow, gypsy, and angel. They thanked her and scrambled off the porch.

She stared at us four haints. She placed a sucker into each of our bags. We moved out of the way so Mommy could take her turn.

The woman stared at the tall form and said, "Ain't you too old for this?"

Mommy answered, "No, ma'am. I'm big for my age. I'm only thirteen." She was thirty-four.

The woman reluctantly dropped a sucker into her opened poke and shut the door. At almost every house we visited, the tall haint got questioned again and again about her age, but she always gave the same answer.

Soon, each of us had half-full pokes of chewy caramels, juicy bubble gum, and red hot jawbreakers. We'd hit every house in our coal camp.

"We can't go back now," Mommy said. "The best treats are up the road, across the tracks. I hear those people give out whole bags of potato chips and large candy bars. It can't get any better than that."

We continued up the crowded tracks with a hobo, a Frankenstein, and a mummy. We walked past trick-or-treaters ringing loud cowbells and blowing Halloween horns. Soon we reached the first house.

The young girl who answered the door gave each trick-or-treater a bag of potato chips. At the next house, we got Reese Cups. Next, we got shiny red apples and big oatmeal cookies. Our pokes were heavy by the time we reached the last house, where we got boxes of candy cigarettes and bubble gum cigars. By this time, most of the alleys were empty, except for a few teenagers who stood talking along the tracks.

"I'm tired," Margaret said. "Can we go home now?"

"Me, too," Noah agreed. "I have enough."

"Yes," I chimed in. "Me, too. Let's go home."

Someone ran across the tracks and yelled, "Hey, everybody, if you really want great treats, go to the last camp below the post office. Those people down there let you reach in the bowl and help yourself. I got two handfuls at several houses!"

"Come on," Mommy said. "Let's go."

"No," we said. "We're tired of walking. Let's go home."

"One more camp," she said. "After we fill our bag down there, we'll go home."

"Mommy, it's dark down there. They don't have any street lights," I said.

"We'll be fine. The railroad tracks will guide us, and the lights from the cars will help." She led us away from the streetlights and onto the dark tracks.

We walked past our camp. I couldn't tell if Daddy was home because the alleys were dark. Our camp's only street light had been off for a month. Occasionally, a car passed by, giving us a second or two of light.

Within a minute or so, total blackness surrounded us. We stumbled along the uneven railroad ties. Often, we missed a step and landed in the gravel between the ties. They were sharp and gouged our ankles.

Lights from a passing car showed us the first house. We crossed the road and walked up the steps. We were too tired to yell, "Trick-or-treat," so the big haint did it for us.

The porch light came on, and the door swung open. An elderly lady with a half-full bowl of treats opened the screen door.

Mommy plunged her hand in the bowl and came out with a fistful of candy. We each did the same.

"Upon my word!" the woman screamed and slapped our hands. "Stop that!" We let go and stared at her. Mommy gasped and stood perfectly still.

"Somebody tried the same thing a few minutes ago, and it's not going to happen again. Open your poke, and I will give you a treat," she said.

Mommy opened her poke. We did the same. She gave us one piece of candy, slammed the door, and turned off the light.

We eased our way out of her yard, and Mommy led us to the next house. She paused in front of the gate. "That boy must have been a little wrong. He probably didn't go to that house. Follow me."

We slowly followed her up the steps and listened as she yelled, "Trick-or-treat!"

The door opened. A short man stood there with a small plastic bowl of bubble gum. "I'm about out," he said. "Somebody came through here a few minutes ago and grabbed two handfuls before I could stop him." He put a piece of gum into each poke and closed the door.

"Let's go home," Noah said. "I'm tired."

"Okay," Mommy patted his shoulder. "Let's go. We have enough."

There was no sign of anyone else out. Only us. No passing cars, no Halloween horns, no bells. The only sound was creek water trickling in front of the houses.

Mommy led us up the alley and across a small bridge. "We're not going to walk the tracks," she said. "We'll walk on the other side, behind those houses near the woods."

"Mommy, that'll take longer," I said. "It's darker over there, too."

"Come on. This way beats the tracks," she said. "We'll be home before you know it. No more stumbling in those gravels or taking a chance of getting egged from pranksters." She led us across the road and behind a row of houses. Lights from a passing car showed that we were entering a small field of weeds with houses and woods on either side.

"Watch your step," she said. "Stay behind a few feet. I'll stomp the weeds a little."

That wasn't too reassuring for me. We were roaming around in complete darkness until a passing car gave us a second or two of light. Other than that, we could not see our hands in front of our faces.

We followed behind her: Margaret, Noah, me. A few seconds later Margaret wailed, "Ouch!" Something struck me!"

Before I could get to her, Noah whimpered, "Ooooo, something's crawling on my face."

I heard a soft thud and Mommy's scream.

"What is it? What's wrong?" I said. I stood still, not knowing who to help first.

"I fell into a big ditch," she sobbed.

Margaret and Noah both cried. I quickly removed the large shirt and head wrap from Noah and brushed him down. "That was only an old spider web," I said. "You're okay."

Margaret Ann's shirt sleeve was caught on a thorny bush. I removed the shirt and jerked it free from the limb. Mommy's wails grew louder.

"You two stand right here. I need to help Mommy."

"I'm coming," I said, easing down into a wide ditch. "Where are you hurt?"

"I'm not hurt. It's my candy." Headlights from a car allowed me to see her searching through leaves on the ground.

She was crying. "I busted my poke when I fell. I've lost my candy. Help me find it." Her hands frantically searched through the leaves.

We found most of the candy. I used my sister's head wrap as a new bag for Mommy and helped her climb out of the ditch. Someone from one of the houses must have heard the commotion and switched on their back porchlight. It shined only enough light to help me see a path to the main road.

I took off my large shirt, tied all the candy pokes inside, and slung it over my shoulder. "Come on," I said. "Follow me. We'll walk up the main road, and we'll be home soon."

Without a word, Mommy followed me, just as I used to follow her.

When we got home, Daddy was glaring at the large hole in the wall. He wore the biggest frown I had ever seen.

"What happened here?" he said pointing toward the hole. He stared directly at Mommy.

Mommy picked up the cut out and placed it over the hole. "I needed soot to blacken our faces for Halloween," she said. "I'll fix it back. Besides, this room needs new wallpaper."

Daddy looked straight into her eyes. "I can't believe you'd do a thing like this," he said, pointing at the hole. This just makes more work for me."

Mommy hung her head. "I said I'll help fix it."

Daddy scowled. "We'll have to seal it tight before winter comes. Cold air will seep down from the attic." He stomped out of the room and returned with a roll of black tape.

"I'll seal it tight," she promised. Mommy held the cut out in place and Daddy taped it to the wall.

After a quick bath, we settled down to do our favorite part of Halloween. Each one of us took turns dumping our loot onto the kitchen table. Daddy stayed in the living room, but Mommy sat at the table with us and watched. Eventually she grew quiet.

We separated the pieces into piles: suckers, bubble gums, jaw breakers, caramels and taffies, Mary Janes, Black Jacks, and candy cigarettes. We proudly piled our specialty items together: potato chips, waxed red lips, candy bars, apples, and cookies. After the inspection was complete, it was time to trade. Mommy seemed to be far off somewhere and only offered a hint of a smile when someone touched her arm or showed her a special treat.

Not sure if we trusted each other, we acted like sneaky squirrels hiding nuts for the winter. We each took turns hiding our candy treasures in the house, making sure no one saw where we put them. Sometime later that evening, Mommy hid her candy, too. At least that's what I thought she was doing. She must have been searching for the right spot from all the bumping and thumping coming from the back bedroom. She never did join Daddy and us kids for TV time, so when the sounds stopped coming from the bedroom, I checked on her. She was in bed.

Prayer Time

Dear God,

I told you The Blue Goose was useless and ugly, and I was ashamed to be seen riding in him. He was worn out and Daddy couldn't keep him running any more. But now that The Goose's gone, I miss him. He worked so hard for our family, and I believe that you sent him to us for a reason.

Daddy is fifty-five and has diabetes. He is sick most of the time. I guess he won't be able to haul coal or gather scrap iron much longer. Mommy is only thirty-six, but she gets around really good. She still looks at her pink square dancing outfit. I believe she really wants to go somewhere, but I'm not sure where. And she keeps singing "O Lonesome Me "and "I'm So Lonesome I Could Cry." I wish I could sing like her.

God, why don't Mommy and Daddy ever hug? Debbie's parents do. All my parents ever talk about are how to pay the bills or repair the house. I can't figure out why we can't live like other people. Did anyone else cut up a wall so their kids could go Trick or Treating?

Thank you for the old blue Ford Daddy drove home. The car looks better than The Goose, but it smokes so much, and it backfires. Daddy told Mommy he put the title in a dead uncle's name to keep the Welfare from cutting us off again. I hate all these secrets. I wonder if Mommy does too. She hasn't talked much since Halloween.

Thank you for taking care of us again.
Kathy

Winter Morning

December sneaked in a little snow. I peered through the ice-covered window at the fresh white layer. Only a dusting lay on the ground before I'd gone to bed, but now there were five or six inches. I tiptoed to the kitchen and turned off the alarm just before it sounded. I eased my way back into bed, not wanting to wake anyone. I was hoping for a snow day. Mommy and Margaret Ann slept across from me and Noah shared a bed with Daddy in the other bedroom.

"Kathy, is that the alarm?" Daddy rolled over on his squeaky bed.

"Yes." I turned on the transistor radio and held it against my ear. The DJ read the scores from last night's high-school game. I didn't have to tune in a station. I left it tuned to WLOG, out of Logan, West Virginia.

Following the scores, there was an advertisement for a local hardware store and an invitation to grocery shop at the A & P, "Where prices can't be beat." Finally, we heard what I'd been waiting for. "An announcement just in from Logan County Schools. There *is* school in Logan County, and the buses are running on the regular schedule."

I turned off the radio and pulled the patch quilt up close around my neck to snuggle for five more minutes.

"Kathy, are you up?" Daddy said. "You're gonna miss the bus."

"I'm up." I threw back the quilt. My feet did not like the cold linoleum any more than I did.

Mommy rolled over and buried beneath her blanket. Margaret's head barely peeped out. They had two more hours of sleep left. Lucky them.

I hurried to the bathroom and turned on the faucet. Nothing came out. I turned on the bath faucet. Same thing. No water. Frozen pipes.

I hurried into the kitchen. I removed one metal tray of ice cubes from the freezer and dumped them into an aluminum pot. Next, I turned on the stove and set the pot over the flame. I tried to be quiet, but it was too late. Daddy had heard me dump the cubes.

"Kathy, what are you doing?"

"Melting ice cubes so I can wash my face."

He strapped on his peg leg, grabbed his coat from the hook on the wall, and came into the kitchen.

"No need to do that. Get your coat. Let's go outside."

I didn't want to go outside. It was cold out there. Our house was the only one in the row that wasn't underpinned. Daddy still couldn't afford it. It sat two feet off the ground, supported by concrete blocks. In the winter, icy cold winds blew underneath the floor and whistled inside through the cracks in the floor and walls.

I turned off the stove and grabbed my coat.

Daddy retrieved the blowtorch and a flashlight from the tool closet. "Open up that faucet," he said, pointing to the sink.

I did and followed him outside. The cold air turned my breath into a white vapor.

We walked to the corner of the house, turned down the side, and stood in front of the kitchen window. He bent down as low as he could, balanced on his good leg, and held the peg leg out to the side. He shone the flashlight on the rag-wrapped pipes and followed them with the light beam. The pipes rose out of the ground and forked in several different directions.

I shivered in the early morning air. I thought about my ice cubes, probably melted by now. I wanted to tell him that we didn't need to come outside. I wanted to tell him I was cold, but I stayed silent.

Daddy's gaze searched the pipes that ran to the kitchen, to the junk room that held the hot water heater, and to the bathroom. For several minutes, he traced the pipes that ran horizontally and vertically under the wooden floor. When we'd moved in, all the pipes were exposed. I remembered when Daddy and I wrapped the pipes with several layers of rags to prevent them from freezing. This past July, we worked in dog-day weather and added the latest wrapping. Now, here we were in frigid December, trying to find the frozen pipe.

I knelt beside my Daddy and searched the pipes. I hoped to find what we were looking for. I wanted to go back inside. I needed to get dressed and pack my things for school.

Daddy bent lower and lay down in the snow. A few flurries swirled around us, chilling me to the bone. He shone the light higher up, under the floor rafters.

"There it is," he said. "It's over there in the middle. See that naked pipe running back to the water tank? It must be frozen back there."

My eyes followed the flashlight to the middle of the house. I saw a long section of pipe that had somehow lost its rags. Or, maybe, in our haste this summer, we may have forgotten to wrap that section.

"Here," he said, lighting the torch. "Now, you have to be real careful with this. Do you hear me? This thing will set the house on fire if you don't do what I say. Don't get the flame near those rags."

I nodded. Daddy turned a knob on the side and adjusted the flame. He let it burn down for a few seconds.

"I want you to crawl up to that pipe, real easy. Keep this flame away from everything. Do you hear me?"

"Yes."

"Don't let it touch anything. I mean nothing."

"Okay." I took hold of the handle. It was the size of a Kool-Aid pitcher and heavier than I'd thought. I'd watched Daddy use the torch before, but this was my first time.

"Now, when you get up there, lightly—very lightly—wave the end of the torch over the pipe, only the part of the pipe that's exposed. Be careful, and don't touch any of the rags with the flame. They'll burn just as quick as dried leaves. You understand?"

"Yes."

It was difficult to crawl on one elbow and drag the torch with the other arm. The air was cold. The wind blew from the front porch to the back and everywhere in between.

"Careful, now," he reminded me.

I crawled across a bed of frozen dirt embedded with small rocks and sticks. A few times, my nightgown snagged on something. If I lifted my head too far, I bumped my head on the wooden floor joists.

Nothing in the neighborhood stirred. No dogs, no cars, no people. The only sounds were my heavy breathing and the whoosh of the flaming torch. Soon I arrived at the naked spot. Daddy held the flashlight on the pipes.

"Okay, I'm here," I said.

"Let the torch sit on the ground. Rest your arm for a minute," he said. "You'll need good arm strength to lift it." I gladly rested the blowtorch on the ground, carefully turning the flame away from me.

"Now," he began, "lightly wave the torch over the pipe. Don't let the flame rest on it for more than a second or two. If you do, you'll burst the pipe."

I waved the torch once, twice. Nothing happened.

"Wave it again. This time listen for it to break loose," he said.

My arms felt heavy, like stiff logs. I lifted the torch one more time and carefully waved the flame across the pipe and listened.

The inside of the pipe cracked. Water splashed in the sink above me.

"I hear it," I said. "Water's running in the sink."

"Turn that little knob all the way to the right and kill the flame," he said. "Now, hurry out of there. The bus will be here in a few minutes."

I barely had enough time to wash my face and brush my teeth before the bus horn tooted. That signaled the lower camp, where we lived. The bus turned at the end of the upper camp and came back to my stop. I pulled on a skirt and sweater and brushed my hair. I grabbed my books and coat and hurried to meet the bus as it pulled in.

I wondered for a moment how many other kids at my school had been under their houses thawing pipes in the cold frigid morning air.

Growing Up

Dear God,

I know I shouldn't have done this, but today I thought about all the womanly neighbors and wanted to know what it would be like to be grown up. They seem to have so much fun driving around in their own cars and hanging out with their boyfriends.

I want to feel that way.

I sneaked a bra out of Mommy's dresser drawer and tried it on. Then I grabbed two apples from the kitchen and put one in each cup. I put on my blouse and stared in the mirror, turning to the left and to the right.

But God, I didn't feel any different.

Kathy

Thirteen

I awakened to a world of red and white. A fluffy white snow covered our house and yard. Red stains on the sheets startled me when I threw back the covers. Slowly, I removed the sheets and took them to the kitchen, where Mommy was doing laundry. I was surprised to see her up so early, since she came home late last night. Daddy and she sat at the kitchen table and whispered for a long time after we'd gone to bed.

During the winter, washday was Saturday or Monday, depending on the weather. Cold temperatures forced us to hang our wet clothes on ropes strung across the bedrooms. Since it took two days for the clothes to dry, a Saturday wash guaranteed dry clothes for school on Monday.

"Why did you roll these up?" she asked. "They won't fit in the washer like this."

I didn't have time to answer. She unrolled the large ball. Suddenly, she stopped unrolling and put the sheets on the floor. She removed a white plastic pan from under the sink. She filled it with cold water and added the sheets. She closed the washer lid and pushed the lever to start the agitator. The old gray Maytag made a sudden jerk as the agitator kicked in and began churning the load.

"These need to soak a while," she said, putting the pan in the sink.

Mommy poured a cup of coffee and sat down at the kitchen table, motioning for me to sit across from her. She removed a calendar from the wall, slid it toward me and pointed to one of the blank spaces.

"You have to write 'Started sick here' on this block," she said. "This is the day you started."

I reluctantly took the pencil she offered and wrote in the empty space on the third Saturday. I wrote the words tiny—very tiny.

"Now, when you finish, you have to write that down, too." She pointed to another block about three or four days away. "In that block, you write 'Finished sick here.' And don't ever forget the day you started. You'll need to know it one day." I looked at the calendar. *December* it said. Just *December*.

I got up to hang the calendar back on the wall, but her hand on my arm stopped me. "There's more," she said. "Sit down. There's a whole lot more."

More? My heart pounded, but I sat down next to her.

"Now that you're *that way*, there's a few things you need to know. First of all, stay away from boys."

Why? I didn't ask.

Mommy took a sip of coffee. "Don't ever let a boy touch you, especially if you are that way."

Touch me where? Or how? I didn't have a chance to ask.

"As soon as the weather clears, we'll go into town and buy a couple of black skirts. You have to wear black when you're this way. The blood won't show if you leak through."

My head hurt and my face burned. I didn't want to hear anymore. I wanted to be somewhere else. Yesterday or last month would have been fine.

"And another thing," she continued, "you won't be able to make a meringue. They'll fail every time. Don't even come in the kitchen if I'm making one. Egg whites won't stiffen when you're that way."

I wanted to leave the table, to run, but I knew better. I had to listen until she finished.

"Now, also remember that you can't mop when you're like this. It will stop the flow, and you'll start all over again and go even longer."

I thought about this for a second or two. "But what if I wear shoes?" I asked.

"It doesn't matter," she said. "No mopping. And no baths. Never take a bath when you're like this. It'll make you stop, and you'll start again in a day or so. It messes up your cycle. Don't bathe."

Mommy refilled her coffee cup. "Oh, yeah, I almost forgot about the cucumbers."

"Cucumbers?"

"You'll kill them. If you're that way, and you walk into a garden where there are cucumbers, you'll kill the vine. The farmer won't get nary a cucumber."

What horrible thing had happened to me? I was dying real slow. Someone had cut me and left me to die. Or was I in shock? I'd heard of people being in shock. Was this what it was like?

"Is that all?" I asked.

"Yeah, pretty much," she answered. "Remember not to get chilled, though. That's the big thing. Chillin' slows you down. And you don't want that."

"Okay." I stood, resisting the urge to run.

"I have a box on the bathroom shelf," she said. "Do you want me to show you?"

I'd seen those things before, had an idea of what they were for and how they were used. I couldn't bear the thought of Mommy explaining it to me, or—God forbid—showing me. "No. I know where they are."

She dumped the rest of the coffee in the sink and grabbed a package of beans from the cabinet. I went to the bathroom, coming out later to sit by the fire in the living room.

From the back room, Margaret and Noah squealed. They'd awakened and had seen the new-fallen snow. From all the commotion, I suspected they were getting ready to go sleigh riding. Soon I heard kids out front, pulling makeshift sleds and plastic pieces through the alley to the mountain.

From the open door, I watched my brother and sister gather pieces of plastic from under the porch while their friends waited.

"Hurry up, sis," Noah called. "Let's be the first ones down the hill."

"I can't," I said. "I'm sick."

For several minutes, I sat close to the fire and watched the flames climb the back of the gas stove.

No boys, no cucumbers, no sledding.

My life was over.

I was thirteen.

A few weeks passed and brought us a new year—1966. It also brought me two black skirts from Jerry's Used Clothing in downtown Logan. I hated wearing those black skirts. I didn't see other girls wearing black, so in the spring, I stopped wearing them. Mommy didn't notice because she seemed occupied, but I couldn't figure out what it was. She didn't laugh as much or cut up with the neighbors like she usually did. I guessed she was still sore at Daddy for scolding her about cutting up the wall at Halloween.

By summer and all during my eighth grade year, Mommy was gone more than usual. Daddy always gave me the same answer: she was ironing up the road for coal miners; she was cleaning house for an elderly lady down the road; or she was down the street visiting neighbors.

I didn't see any new clothes or many home improvements made during this time with Mommy's money she was supposed to be earning. But one day I came home and smelled wallpaper paste from Daddy's room she'd papered that morning. The paper was green with a circus theme. She hung it wrong and the acrobats hung in the wrong direction and circus animals floated upside down. When I did finally get to talk to her, I mentioned the wallpaper. She said, "It doesn't matter how it goes up, just so it's clean." But it mattered to me. How could I ever invite a friend over with roaches running everywhere, worn out rugs and upside down wallpaper? It seemed like my dream of inviting a friend over was never going to happen.

Where's Mommy?

Dear God,

Thank you for my summer job. I'm glad to be earning money now that I'm fourteen. Everything is all right with this. But something is not right with Mommy. She's always gone when I come home. And when she is home, she doesn't laugh or cut-up like she used to. She and Daddy don't sit at the table anymore figuring out bills or making plans to fix things around the house.

Daddy keeps saying the same thing—she's doing laundry somewhere. But everyone is already in bed, and she's still not home. I fixed supper again tonight.

Her fancy pink blouse and matching skirt are not on the rod. I thought she told me that she only wore it when she goes dancing. Am I the only one that notices she's gone most of the time?

Kathy

American Bandstand

In September 1967, I entered my last year in junior high as a 9th grader. I enjoyed school, as I always had, and looked forward to each day. I liked my classmates, and they liked me. But when time came to share things about home life, I stayed silent. I hoped no one connected me to Daddy if they saw him begging on the street. Although we were on Welfare, the checks were small. Our family couldn't live without somehow bringing in extra income. I still didn't invite anyone to spend the night because of the terrible condition of the inside and outside of the house. And there wasn't any extra money for pop or snacks. But I was hopeful that one day things would get better.

Margaret was in the 5th grade and Noah was in the 3rd. I was thankful for my summer job at Verdunville Grade School where I served snacks to summer school students. I used my earnings to buy a few new school clothes and saved a little for extra paper and pencils. I still hadn't seen much of Mommy. She was gone almost all the time, and when she did come home it was late at night after we had gone to bed. When I mentioned it to Daddy, he still said she was working. I often wondered if he was keeping something from us kids.

On a chilly Saturday in October I got up early to begin chores, hoping I would finish in time to watch one of my favorite TV shows. I wasn't quite finished, but I turned on the TV to *American Bandstand*. Dick Clark stood next to two teenagers.

The tune ended, and Dick Clark held a microphone close to the young lady's face. "And what do you want to rate this record, Lisa?"

"I kinda liked it, because it was easy to dance to. I give it an eighty-five," Lisa said.

I stopped mopping and turned to look at the face that went with Lisa.

"And what about you, Todd? What did you think of the new song?"

"I definitely liked the beat, and everyone seemed to enjoy the music, so I give it a ninety."

"All right," Dick said. "Eighty-five and ninety averages out to be eight-seven and a half, which is a pretty good score for a new song."

I dipped the mop into the bleach water and wrung it out. Somehow, I always ended up mopping during *American Bandstand*, which I didn't always get to watch. Chores came first. Daddy had relaxed a bit about hiding the TV so much. He felt we could trust our neighbors, and the investigators didn't come around so often anymore. They sent papers in the mail, instead.

I couldn't stare at the screen all the time. I always stopped and listened to the special guests and Rate-A-Record. I mopped even harder and faster during the Clearasil and Spearmint commercials.

That day, the house was quiet, especially for a Saturday. Usually, Mommy was up by nine o'clock, if she was home, but that day I didn't see her before ten. The coffee she so dearly loved hadn't perked in the pot, and she hadn't turned on the *Saturday Morning Country Countdown*. She stayed in the back room. Occasionally, a thump or bump would sound, making me think she was rearranging the furniture in the bedroom, which caused me to think twice before going back there. I didn't want to spend the rest of my day cleaning. I'd wait until after my show to talk with her.

Noah and Margaret, now eight and ten, usually tracked through my freshly mopped rooms once or twice. Today, they never tracked a single step. I looked out the window to see if they were in the front yard. They weren't.

Dick Clark seated himself in the audience between two beautiful people and announced his special guest. I heard part of the introduction before I ran to the kitchen and dumped the mop water into the sink. I hung the mop on a nail on the back porch and called for my brother and sister again. Still no answer. This didn't overly concern me because when they didn't answer, they were always out front, beyond the bushes, playing in the sand that washed down the alley.

I ran dishwater into the porcelain sink and gathered the morning's few breakfast dishes. Daddy had already eaten, and the plate he'd left on the table beside his coffee cup was streaked with yellow from two fried eggs and speckled with crumbs from toast prepared under the oven broiler. Two empty cereal bowls told me the munchkins had eaten and run. They would come bounding in soon, begging for a peanut butter sandwich.

Daddy's felt hat and jacket were not on the hook near the door. He was doing what he usually did on Saturdays. Begging. Since he'd traded The Goose for the automatic, it was easier for him to drive. Now that I was fifteen, I still went with him occasionally to sell ink pens, but today, I had stayed home to do chores.

The songs played on. Occasionally, during slow songs, I stopped and waltzed around the kitchen with the broom. I preferred doing the twist, because I didn't need a partner. It was easy to do.

I finished the dishes and sat down to watch the rest of the show. A car horn sounded out front. I parted the curtains. A Black Diamond Taxi waited in front of the house. The driver looked straight at me and motioned.

"Mommy," I called. "There's a taxi blowing out front. Want me to tell him he's got the wrong house?"

She didn't answer. A few more thumps came from the bedroom.

I opened the front door. Cool October air rushed past me. I stared through the screen and motioned the driver to go, but he didn't. Footsteps sounded behind me, and I turned around.

Mommy came into the room wearing one of her better dresses and a thin black jacket. A flowered scarf wrapped around her head and tied under her chin. She held a brown suitcase in one hand, her Stanley guitar in the other.

"Where'd you get the suitcase?" I asked. We didn't own one.

Mommy ignored me and pushed past to the screen door. She waved to the driver and sat the guitar and suitcase on the floor.

"Where ya going?" I asked.

She turned to me, placed her hands on my shoulders and looked down. Then she looked straight into my face. She swallowed hard, her eyes teary. "I'll be seeing you," she whispered. She quickly picked up the suitcase and guitar and hurried through the door.

"Mommy!" I yelled. "Where ya going?"

She didn't answer, and she didn't look back. She walked out the door to the waiting taxi.

The driver slung the suitcase and guitar into the backseat and opened the front door. Mommy climbed inside.

I spotted Margaret and Noah as they looked up from the sand they were playing in. "Mommy! Mommy!" they yelled.

The taxi driver closed her door and walked around the car and got inside. Mommy was inside. *My Mommy!*

My brother and sister left the sand pile and ran toward the passenger door. "Mommy, can I go? Take me!"

Mommy sat straight and tall in the front seat. She never turned to wave or even glance at the kids or me.

I joined my brother and sister in the alley as the taxi pulled away. We watched as it disappeared around the curve. I wasn't sure what to say, but I put my arms around them and told them she was going into town and would be back later. That satisfied them enough to go back to their sand pile.

When Daddy came home that evening, I met him at the door. "Daddy, Mommy left in a taxi today."

He walked past me, tossed a sock of coins on the kitchen table, and without a word, walked into his bedroom. My crippled Daddy threw himself across the bed and laid there like a Raggedy Ann doll. That was the only time I'd ever seen him cry. It broke my heart. Up to this point, I wasn't sure what to believe about Mommy leaving in the taxi. Where was she going?

But after hearing his loud sobs, I knew it was serious. In between sobs, he blubbered something about, "I did the best I could.... Oh God, what more could I have done?" I realized this was what others referred to as "my Mommy ran away." But I wanted to know why.

Margaret and Noah heard Daddy's wails and came running into the bedroom. They bent over and asked, "Daddy, what's wrong?" in between sniffles. They were scared. They had never seen him this sad.

He never moved out of his position: hands clasped above his head and his forehead pressed on top. The rest of his body lay limp with his peg leg and other leg hanging over the bed a few inches. His shoulders and back jerked in between heavy sobs. I stood at the end of the bed while Margaret and Noah climbed on—one on each side of him. They patted his back and shoulders. "Don't cry, Daddy," one of them said. "Daddy, it's okay. You'll be all right." They didn't know what had happened; still they tried to console him.

I didn't cry. I was numb.

The sorrowful sight snapped me back to the moment. It finally sank in that Mommy had run away. The roles of Mother and housekeeper had dropped into my lap. I rubbed Daddy's back and hugged Margaret and Noah.

"Hey, you know what," I said trying to sound brave. "It's going to be okay. I'll take care of us. I can cook and wash clothes." And I meant it.

A little later Daddy got up and washed his face with cold water. He walked slower than usual and looked lost. Margaret and Noah asked several questions about her whereabouts, but Daddy answered, "She's gone." After a bit, he went to bed and slept. The kids and I tiptoed through the house, so we wouldn't wake him up.

Later that night, before bed, I looked around the house to see what Mommy had taken in her suitcase. The pink square dancing outfit, all of her songbooks, her white mixing bowl with red tulips, and some pictures from the photo box were gone. I got the kids ready for bed, locked the doors, and went to bed. I lay there thinking how I didn't know what I felt. Empty? Lost? Afraid? I knew that I needed sleep, though, because the next day, Sunday, I had a lot to do to get three of us ready for school, do homework, and check on our food supply. I went from being a daughter and sister to a Mother in the time it took for my mother to pack a bag and climb into a taxi, never looking back.

I had one more jolting thought. Had Mommy given Daddy hints that she was leaving? Her always admiring her pink dancing outfit and singing songs about being lonesome—were those hints that I missed? Maybe this explained why she was gone so much. She was trying to distance herself from us, so it would be easier for her to leave. What could be the reason that she actually walked out on us?

Rosa with Margaret, Noah and Kathy

Rosa and Kathy, shortly before Rosa left in a taxi

Decorating

Dear God,

I miss Mommy. I wonder where she went. These past few weeks have been hard since she left. Daddy talked to a few of her friends, but they didn't know anything.

I've been thinking about Mommy and Daddy. He's 56 and doesn't feel well most days. Mommy was 37, full of fun, and got around quicker than a Jack in the Box. Was he too old for her?

Is she dancing in the pink outfit now? Is that what she needed to do? Daddy won't talk about her. I'm trying hard to be brave, but there's so much work to do, and I'm missing out. I don't have much free time. I'd love to walk the tracks with Debbie or watch the boys play baseball in the field behind her house.

Oh well, maybe I'd feel a little better if we had money to decorate. I can't stand these upside-down gazebos and southern belles anymore. Why did Mommy hang this wallpaper upside down like she did the acrobats in the other room?

Margaret and I want a pink bedspread and curtains now that we share the same bedroom. I hate those fifty cent plastic curtains. The flowers disappear more each time we wash them.

And...we have too many Jesus calendars. We have Jesus walking on water, Jesus knocking at the door, Jesus holding the baby lamb, and Jesus praying in the garden. I'll keep Jesus on the cross, because that one says it all. And I'll keep the angel watching those children walk across the bridge and Mother Mary with that heart necklace. Mother Mary, mother to Jesus and us all.

I'll keep one calendar with the almanac. We use that as a guide for everything, God; even wallpapering. Maybe my wallpaper cracked in here because Mommy papered in the wrong phase of the moon. Maybe that's why the kraut rotted in the jars. It was canned in the wrong sign.

I'd also like to have covers for the couch and chair and a new linoleum rug. A table lamp would be nice, so we can see each other at night. We don't have even one lamp, God. Maybe with the living room looking halfway decent, I could invite a friend over.

I can't decorate any more tonight, God. I'm too sleepy. I'll talk to you again tomorrow.

Love,
Kathy

It Will Be Good for You

I checked the front alley for signs of the kids playing. I spotted them near the old blue 1957 Ford Daddy had gotten recently after he'd sold The Goose for scrap. He gave the man at the junk yard something in addition to make the trade more even. Wherever we went, the Ford backfired all the time and smoked so much it looked like we were on fire. We always got lots of stares from people sitting on their porches or walking on the road when we passed by.

There would *never* be another Goose. I'd spent many hours in that truck with Daddy. I was surprisingly saddened when it fell apart after having it for nearly eighteen years. Satisfied that the kids were okay, I returned to the kitchen.

The clock hand neared six in the evening. I swiped the table with the dishrag as water gurgled down the drain. I hurried. Tons of homework waited for me, and my gym suit needed ironing. I reached for the broom. I didn't like my recent evening schedule since Mommy left, but I had to do it. I'd much rather be talking to Debbie and her older sisters about fashion and makeup. And, of course, boys.

"Come here," Daddy said through the doorway. "It's time for the news. I want you to see something."

"In a minute." I didn't have time for the news. The kitchen needed sweeping, and I needed to do homework.

Daddy found used TV tubes, and he now watched the news every night. I didn't have to sit behind the set anymore and watch for faulty tubes. Every night for the past week, Daddy called me promptly at six-thirty to get in there.

I swept the crumbs from beneath the table with hard, fast strokes, flinging them into the dustpan. I rinsed the suds down the drain and threw the dishrag across the faucet. I stepped through the doorway that connected the living room with the kitchen.

"Sit down," Daddy said. "Watch the news. Learn something about the world. That's the only way you're gonna know anything."

I wanted to sit down; I'd have loved it. But I couldn't. Ever since Mommy ran away, I hadn't been able to sit at all. I cleaned house, washed clothes, and cooked meals. I helped care for my eight-year-old brother and ten-year-old sister. I was fifteen and the woman of the house. Daddy helped whenever he could, but it was difficult with one leg and one hand. I wanted to make things easier on him because in addition to diabetes, he had been diagnosed with high blood pressure. At times like this, I couldn't help being angry that she had left.

"Welcome to the six-thirty edition of the nightly news," the announcer began. "News from the state, news from the nation, and news from around the world." The screen showed our state's gold-domed capitol, followed by The White House, and finally an image from London. "That's it!" Daddy shouted. He pointed to the screen. "Did you see it? That was Big Ben! It's the biggest clock in the world. People everywhere love to hear that clock chime. Did you know that sailors from all over the world set their clocks to Big Ben?"

"Yeah, I know," I said, turning to leave. "It's real pretty."

"Remember that day in the dump when you found the Roosevelt clock, you said you wanted to see Big Ben?"

I glanced at the clock sitting on top of the Philco radio. "Yes, I remember."

"Go see that clock one day. Don't take my word for it, Katherine. See if it's really there. Then you'll know for sure. It'll be good for you."

"I will," I said. "I'll go someday." I turned to go back in the kitchen.

"Get an education," he said. "Make something of yourself."

I nodded. I needed to get started on my homework, not sit there and daydream about seeing Big Ben. "Okay," I said, to please him.

I had two hours of English and science homework to complete, but first I needed to iron my gym suit. I spread a heavy towel on the kitchen table and plugged in the iron. A wrinkled suit meant a lower gym grade, so I ironed carefully. In addition to ironed, Mrs. Morris required that the collar had to turn back in a particular way around the shoulders, the way a new shirt came packaged. I had practiced so much that I could iron as good as the other girls' mothers ironed. The only thing I couldn't do well was darn a hole. My gym suit had a hole under the arm, and no matter how many times I sewed it, it split every time I raised my arm.

My gym bag was finally ready, complete with a fresh towel, a washcloth, a bar of soap, deodorant, and bath powder. Tomorrow morning, I would definitely get all the supply points required by my gym teacher. I closed the bag and looked at the clock. Already, it read 6:45.

Time for a new chapter in science class. I hated new chapters. The teacher required us to define vocabulary, write the chapter summary and outline the chapter. I sharpened two pencils with a kitchen knife and wrote my name on my paper. I turned to the vocabulary page and groaned. Half the page was missing. My thoughts went back to the beginning of school and the way I scrambled to find used books. I found a good deal when I bought all my books for ten dollars from another student.

I'd saved Daddy money, but now I stared at the list of vocabulary words. There were supposed to be twenty, but I counted only seven. I hadn't noticed that when I bought the book. I wrote down the first word and looked at the clock. I looked at the words again and back at the clock. I flipped to the end of the chapter to look at the summary. I groaned. There were fifteen summary sentences. Homework would take forever. I'd be here all night.

Within minutes, I grew tired. I didn't feel like copying words, phrases, and sentences for the next two hours. The teacher took up our pages, gave us a checkmark if we had it, and a zero if we didn't. My jaw clenched. I wanted nothing more than to go to bed and sleep and sleep.

I closed the science book, deciding to do it last. I moved on to the English assignment. I might feel better if I could at least get that one out of the way.

I opened my folder and read the assignment. "Write a two-page essay titled 'What I Want to be When I Grow Up.'" I pulled two sheets of paper out of my notebook and stared at the blank space.

The refrigerator kicked off. The kitchen was silent. I thought and thought. What do I want to be when I grow up? I tried to see myself being grown up and working at a real job. I couldn't see anything through the uncertain fog in my head.

The silence broke when Daddy opened the front door. He called my brother and sister to come inside. They begged for more playtime. After a few minutes, I heard bathwater running and the soft thump of someone digging clothes out of the bedroom closet. A little later, low voices came from the TV. My brother and sister had settled down on the couch with Daddy. I looked at the title I'd penciled at the top of my page. "What I Want to Be When I Grow Up."

I looked at my raggedy science book and my worn and faded gym bag. Someday, I thought, I will have time for TV, for the news, even for Big Ben. I picked up my pencil and with utter clarity, I began to write.

I don't know what I want to be when I grow up, but I know one thing for sure: I don't want to be poor.

A Letter from Mommy

dear kathy john family and all

how are you, fine I hope. well, I have been keeping pretty busy here in ohio. I have cleaned the upstairs and downstairs, and basement too. I took out all the newspapers and laid them in the coon cage and fed the squirrels fresh nuts in the backyard. this morning I set down to all the good orange juice that I could drink and a big breakfast of bacon, eggs, gravy, toast, and jelly. It was so good that I keep eating and eating. my belly swelled and swelled because I was so full. yesterday for sunday dinner, I fried two big chickens, mashed potatoes, and made gravy and biscuits. I also fixed a lemon pie and a chocolate one too. everything was so good and it all was eaten real fast. well, how is the family? I hope you are fine. how is tiger? he sure was a pretty cat. are you feeding him every day? remember that he likes that cat food in the green box. be sure to remember now. he won't eat nothing else. well, saturday me and tom went to big bear and bought ten pounds of butter, three big packs of pork chops, two giant boxes of tide, and all kinds of other stuff. we like to go there when they have sales. you should see my freezer down in the basement. its loaded so full it looks like its going to fly away. I dont believe I can get another pack of chicken in there. well you all be good. I am going to close so I can go play my guitar. that's all I ever get done around here is running up and down these stairs. I never get time to play my guitar. even if I go hide up in the sunroom, they find me and want me to do something—clean the coon cage, vacuum the stairs—you name it, they want me to do it. but this time I am going to fool them. I am taking the guitar and me down to the basement where no one will find us.

love from mommy . . . .

This letter arrived several months after Mommy ran away. Up until this time, we did not know where she was. I was surprised to hear that she went north to Ohio, since several of the neighbors commented she had probably headed south to Nashville to pursue country music. But I was more surprised about her mentioning going to the store with Tom. We never knew anyone named Tom. Who was he? I wonder if Daddy knew him. But Daddy never discussed her leaving, and I never questioned him.

Several more letters followed, basically saying the same thing. All were addressed exactly the same, written mostly in lower case, and all lacked punctuation. Daddy always had me to read the letter to him. Afterward he'd say, "Burn it!" Margaret and Noah's only comments were, "When's she coming home? Did she say? Why didn't she tell us?"

The letters were painful to read, and I hated to watch his face when I read the parts about her having so much great food or going places with Tom. Or the mention that Tom brought out his fiddle and played along with her while she played the guitar.

It was cruel enough for her to abandon us, but it was more difficult for me when she described how good she had it. Could she not remember how we struggled for food and other comforts every month? After reading the third or fourth letter, it occurred to me that she thought she was someone who was writing to her sister or cousin, not to her children and husband.

Suddenly, I felt pity for her. And I was more determined than ever to get an education and get as far away from poverty as I could.

All Men Are Not Created Equal

Ninth grade had been going great until one day Mommy's leaving a few months before had finally sunk in. All the extra chores and caring for the family had worn me down. I couldn't wait to get home.

The old school bus creaked along, getting closer to my stop. Mr. Browning, my ninth-grade civics teacher, who I always respected, taught something in class that angered me. It was the first time in my fifteen years that I had ever known a teacher to tell a lie.

The bus rolled to an abrupt stop at the railroad crossing in front of the Island Creek Store. Beside the company store was my destination, the Verdunville Post Office. I needed to be alone.

Gracie, our bus driver, flagged the kids who lived behind the company store across the road. She watched them as they hurried across the railroad tracks. Today, I did not follow the others across the tracks. Instead, I headed toward the post office below the store. A couple of other students followed.

I shifted my literature and civics books in the cradle of my arms and hurried to the little brown building. The flag flapped in front of the post office as I walked by. The other students went inside to get their family's mail, but I walked around the side of the building to the back. I sat on the ground and stared at the rusty, sudsy creek. I found the page in the civics book that had angered me:

> "We hold these truths to be self-evident, that all men are

> *created equal, that they are endowed by their Creator with certain inalienable Rights; that among these are Life, Liberty and the pursuit of Happiness."*
>
> —Thomas Jefferson,
> *The Declaration of Independence, July 4, 1776*

Tears filled my eyes. Happiness? How could all men be created equal, when some people had food and some didn't? Why did our family always run out of food the last week of every month? All around me, people ate sandwiches on their porches every day of the year. Why did my Mommy run away and not somebody else's? How was I supposed to be happy when hunger was frequent and I had to work even harder to keep up with being in Mommy's place and trying to get through school? Where was the happiness for me?

I folded my arms across my chest. I closed my eyes and mumbled several times, "All men are *not* created equal!" I remained on the ground for a few more minutes trying to figure it out.

Daddy often spoke of how the Cooks next door afforded many luxuries, including vacations, because Mr. Cook was a coal miner. "They make about eight-hundred dollars a month," he said. "And now, take the Thompsons across the street there. That family gets about three-hundred dollars a month from Social Security. They can buy all the food they want."

I teared up when I remembered the last part Daddy had said. "We're on welfare, so we only get ninety dollars a month. That doesn't divide very well among a family of five." Not even that now there were four.

Tears rolled down my cheeks. Tears that I had saved up for months. At that moment, it hit me that, in life, everyone was an eight, a three, or a one based on the amount of money they received each month. Our family was a *one*, but only if you rounded ninety dollars up to one hundred. We were less than ones.

I sat there a little longer and thought about the way things were. I was reminded of the paper I had to write about what I wanted to be when I grew up. Although things weren't clear to me how I was going to do it, I did not want to be a one.

A few minutes later, I gathered my books, walked across the tracks to my house, and washed my face. I didn't want Daddy to know I had been crying because he had enough to worry about. After supper, I cleaned the kitchen, did homework, and got Margaret and Noah ready for bed. Later when I went to bed, I pulled back the curtain and stared at the brilliant white moon. It was the same moon that shone on Mommy wherever she was. I thought about who could comfort me now, and it was God. Somehow, things would get better.

Dancing and Dating

At the end of ninth grade, I applied for a summer job with the Logan County Board of Education as part of a cleaning crew. Several teams of us were placed in various schools with the job of cleaning every desk, window, floor, hallway, and bathroom in the school, plus everything else in between. I did not mind the work at all. Actually, I was happy to be earning money that would go toward a better set of books when school started. I never wanted to repeat what happened last year when I bought a set of cheap books with pages missing. Although it saved Daddy money, it was frustrating for me not to be able to do homework.

Our scrub crew was the best and came highly recommended, thanks to our strict, but kind supervisor. "Don't ever leave a dirty mop in any school," Mrs. Vance often said. "Keep your supplies—and yourselves—clean." She expected us to show up for work with brushed hair and clean clothes. If not, she'd be sure to tell us.

One of her most repeated phrases was, "Don't ever be afraid to stand in line on payday. Be proud to stand and reach out your hand to get your paycheck." I have never forgotten that one. Cleaning those schools and keeping up with our house made the summer fly. Mrs. Vance completed the last time sheet and we said our good-byes. I missed her when school started. Though the work was hard, she made it bearable with her sense of humor and by sharing family stories during our lunch period. She made us take time out for lunch, and she made sure that everyone had a sandwich.

Two weeks after my job ended, I entered school as a sophomore. It was 1968, and Mommy had been gone almost a year. She still wrote the same letters saying the same thing every month. I read them to Daddy. Afterward, he'd say, "Burn it!' I never did. I stuffed them in a coffee can and hid it in the attic access above the refrigerator. I'm not sure why I disobeyed him. Maybe I thought she was still with us if I had the letters.

Margaret was in the 6th grade and was doing fine in school. She favored Mommy and had her complexion and slender face. She was shy and stayed near the house. In addition to our own cat, she had grown fond of the neighbors' cats and dogs and sneaked them in the house when Daddy wasn't around. Sometimes Margaret couldn't keep the animals quiet.

Whenever Daddy heard a whimper or a "Meow," he said, "Is there a dog or cat in here? There better not be. Get that animal out of the house. We can barely feed ourselves!" I'd hear a soft thump near Margaret's bedroom window as she pulled back the screen and let the animal out on the porch. I never told on her. Daddy had enough worries, and I figured Margaret enjoyed loving them and letting them love her back.

Noah was beginning 4th grade and was misbehaving in school. The teachers knew Mommy had run away and tried to be understanding, but he kept acting out. Daddy scolded him for climbing out the classroom window and back talking the teacher. After school, he spent most of his time playing in the alleys with friends. Sometimes Daddy called his name several times before he came home. He begged to stay out later each evening. "Please, Daddy! Thirty more minutes, okay?" Noah debated with Daddy every evening, but Daddy always held firm.

I enjoyed all my tenth grade classes and teachers, but I quickly changed my mind from what I thought last year, about people being eights, threes, or ones. Now I was going to school with kids who I thought had to be tens or twelves based on how they dressed. Logan High School was fed by several junior highs, and I had never seen so many beautiful girls' outfits.

I would have given anything to have some of what they wore: poor boy knit tops, hip hugger skirts with wide belts, baby doll dresses, and pink Yardley lipstick. I had never seen so many beautiful plaid skirts with matching pullover sweaters and knee socks. How far did the numbers go? I couldn't figure it out. All I knew was that I was a one based on our income of $90.00 a month. I didn't like it and was convinced that I would not be a one the rest of my life. Thank goodness I borrowed clothes from Debbie which made it look like I had a few more outfits.

To my surprise, I was elected president of my homeroom and secretary of the sophomore class. I also had a part-time job doing clerical work for teachers during my study hall. I earned $25.00 a month from the Logan County Board of Education, which had a program of continuing employment for low-income families of high school students. I was so glad to be chosen for this opportunity, even though it meant less time for me. Not having a study hall meant more homework. Now I was able to buy shampoo, lotion, and other things that Daddy wasn't able to buy, plus help with school supplies. Things were getting a little better, but I couldn't help think about dating and what would I say if someone were to ask me out. I hadn't really talked with anyone about what to do or say, or how to act. Then a wonderful opportunity came out of nowhere.

One Friday night Daddy let me spend the night with Debbie. Her two older sisters were going to a dance at the Rooster's Tail, a place in Logan. Someone said their special lighting made "white" look brilliant, and I had always wanted to see what they meant. After much begging, they agreed to take us only if we heeded their advice.

"Don't stand around like a wallflower," Linda said.

"Okay," we nodded.

"If somebody asks you to dance, say *yes*," Carol added. "No matter who it is or what he looks like, dance."

"That way other boys will see you dancing and they won't be afraid to ask you," Linda added.

I hadn't thought about dancing up to that point because I only knew the twist and the four-corners from watching *American Bandstand*. I was happy just to be going. After all, it was my first time hearing a real band.

Debbie and I sat in the back seat and chatted nervously on the drive to Logan. We speculated on the songs we hoped to hear and assured each other that we looked fine. When we got there, couples and singles filed through the door leading to the dim dance hall. And then I saw the magic! Everyone whose clothing had even the tiniest bit of white stood out from the crowd. They were as noticeable as a flashing neon sign. The thin white stripes in my blouse stood out as well.

It didn't take long for the band to tune up and begin their first song, "Light My Fire" by the Doors. Carol and Linda each got a partner right away and moved to the dance floor along with several couples. Debbie and I stood along a wall with others. The song ended and Carol came over.

"Stop looking scared," she said. "You need to smile."

Debbie and I looked around and smiled. The second song began—a slow one. Immediately, almost everyone went onto the floor, including most of the ones standing along the walls. I was trying hard to identify the name of the song when two boys approached Debbie and me at the same time. One stood in front of her and the other in front of me. Debbie walked away with her guy, and I stood looking into the face of a stringy haired guy with a sheepish grin and broken front tooth. A real winner! He reached his hand out for mine, and I nodded just as I heard the words, "Hey Jude!"

Oh no! A waltz. I had no idea where to put my hands, what to do or how to move. I remembered Carol and Linda's words—*just dance with whoever asks!* Before I had time to think further, the guy put his arms around my back and pulled me real tight up against him. Our midsections seem to blend into one. I could barely breathe. The band played on while my guy continued to press himself into me. When I tried to back up, he held me tighter and pressed harder. I looked at the other couples who seemed to be moving around the floor, actually waltzing. Not us. I had no idea what this was called, but I wanted the song to end. I wanted to go back and stand along the wall...and be a wallflower...and I did after my partner released me. The band played a few more fast songs and my partner strutted all over the floor with a different girl each time.

Then a member of the band said, "Now we're gonna slow it down a bit with one from Percy Sledge."

A few notes sounded from the organ and the vocalist began, *"When a man loves a woman..."* Oh no, another waltz. I saw my partner coming my way, and I ducked behind other people so he wouldn't see me. I'd had enough dancing for the night.

On the drive home, I decided I wasn't going to any more dances unless I went with someone I knew and liked. I wasn't going to throw myself out to just anyone who came along, and I'd be more selective about who put their arms around me. I was going to be in control.

Soon the semester ended and excitement buzzed in our science class. During the second semester, our biology teacher instructed the class on frog dissection. The day before we were to begin, he put us in pairs. A fellow classmate, David, and I were assigned to work together. He was taller than me, quiet, and had blue eyes and sandy hair. Although we had been in class all year, he kept to himself. The only thing I knew about him was that he loved to hunt and fish. Occasionally, he missed an afternoon class or two to go to the mountains or a nearby lake.

Mr. Nichols dipped frogs out of a plastic container and placed them on trays alongside several silver utensils. He handed one of the trays to David, and I picked up the handouts from the front table. I opened the textbook to the page with the frog anatomy, while David pinned the frog on the small absorbent mat. I started to write our names on the lab sheet but realized my pencil lead had broken. I went to the wall sharpener and was about to turn the crank when I heard a whisper from behind me. "Can I take you home today?" I turned, surprised to see that David had followed me.

Ignoring him, I blew on my injection-sharp point and quickly returned to our table. He was cute, but I didn't really know him. I stared at the pinned-down gray-white frog lying on the biology table. I listened to Mr. Nichols, who was still giving instructions. Somehow, I got lost between scalpel instructions and organ identification.

Scalpel in hand, David surveyed the tiny creature and made a cut on his abdomen. Other students were rereading Mr. Nichols's handouts and flipping through their science texts, but David carved our frog, his hands steady and confident. He removed a piece from the frog and placed it on the lab identification sheet. He and I repeated this process a few more times, until we had completed the dissection. We stayed focused on the assignment and rarely spoke. I later wondered if I had made a mistake in turning him down. After all, he was kinda growing on me.

Later in the school year, David again asked me if he could take me home after school. This time, I said *yes*, but all the time wondering how I was going to handle where he could let me out. I surely would not let him pull up to the house.

When the bell rang, I met him in front of the school. We walked to the student parking lot and left in his father's red Volkswagen. At the end of town, he pulled onto the lot of Otis Ratliff's Gulf Station, signaled the attendant, and went inside. David told me his parents were divorced, and that he lived with his grandparents. His mother remarried and moved out of state, but his father remarried and lived close by.

David came out with a package of Teaberry gum. He opened the package and popped a piece into his mouth. He continued doing this until all five sticks were gone. He didn't offer me one stick. I thought he must be nervous or had forgotten that I was there.

During the twenty-minute ride to my house, he played with the radio dials the whole time. I never heard a complete song, because as soon as one came on, he'd change the station.

Once or twice, I spoke up. "That's a good song."

David changed the station.

When we arrived at #16 Camp, I asked him to let me out at the post office. I wasn't sure how Daddy would take it if he saw a boy bringing me home. We smiled and said goodbye to each other, but we talked very little afterward. Absolutely no follow up. I wondered why.

That sophomore year came to an end quickly, and it was time once more to find a summer job. I was going to apply for the scrub crew, but I got lucky. The Logan Board of Education needed a typist for the summer, and I was hired. I was glad to be working again and thankful that I could buy extra treats for Margaret and Noah—sugar cookies, Fritos, and grape soda.

Near the end of July Debbie was waiting for me when I got home from work. She ran to meet me.

"You have to say yes," she said.

"About what?" I asked.

"David wants to take you on a date. Darrell told me this afternoon." Darrell and Debbie had been seeing each other for a few months.

"I don't think so. I don't have time, and I really don't want him seeing the house."

"He can come to our house and pick you up there. He said he'd take you to the movies or the drive-in—anywhere you want to go. Say yes so I can have Darrell to tell David you'll go."

I looked at the blistering paint on the house, the upturned boards on the front porch, and the leaning fence.

"I'll have to think about it," I said.

Juggling It All

I did think about it, but I didn't say yes.

"A boy doesn't care what your house looks like, "Debbie said. "He's coming to see you, not the house!" I still wasn't convinced.

September came and I began the eleventh grade in the secretarial training advanced-placement classes. I was elected homeroom president again. I enjoyed being a leader and working for my classmates. I planned an end-of-the-year trip to Camden Park for the second year in a row and a class picnic at Chief Logan State Park. I really loved my classmates, and I believed they cared for me too.

Evenings were cramped. One bookkeeping problem easily took from two to three hours to complete. Two to three pages of shorthand took a couple hours to transcribe. If there was a story to read in literature or part of a chapter left in social studies, I didn't get into bed until late. I still juggled my evening chores and took care of the kids.

I was so thankful when the Board of Education offered me another part-time job *during* the school year. I took the job of typing and making copies for the shop and vocational teachers at school. I worked for them before school started, during my lunch period, and during study hall. I didn't have much free time, but I was happy to earn money for books and clothes.

Daddy hadn't been feeling too well. His blood pressure and blood sugar both had been high, and now he took medication. Age had crept up on him. He was 58. My active Daddy was slowing down.

A few weeks later, in the autumn of my eleventh-grade school year, who do I see every day when I go down the hall to get my clerical work from the teachers? David. He was taller still, and he offered me his cute smile. We began speaking to each other each morning, and after several October mornings of idle chit chat, David asked me out.

I accepted.

But I declined Debbie's offer to meet at her house. I asked David to drive up the back alley. It was darker out there, and the ugliness wouldn't show as bad.

That same night, I told Daddy that I had a date to go to the movies with a teacher's son. Daddy had great respect for teachers, so I figured that would help my case. I alternated between sweaty palms and breathlessness while I waited for Friday. I did a little bit of house cleaning on Thursday, and a little more on Friday, both to keep myself busy and to lessen my chores on Saturday.

Friday evening came. I was excited and nervous. David had said he'd pick me up at six-thirty—I was sure of it. How else could we be on time for the seven o'clock movie? I parted the curtains once more, and peered up and down the alley. No red Volkswagen, no David, nothing. Seven o'clock came and went. Still no David. So much for a first date, I thought.

I'd almost given up on the idea, when I heard a car in the back alley. David had arrived! I grabbed my sweater and walked out to meet him, hoping I could get away without my brother and sister seeing me. If they did, they would beg to come along, or Margaret might say something embarrassing, *like blurting out about the birthmark on my leg!*

David waved a friendly and shy hello, and he jumped out of the car to meet me at our wooden gate. I let him open the gate and the car door for me. He wore a camouflaged hunting cap and a hunter's vest adorned with burrs. I bent down to enter the car but hesitated. On the back seat, stretched out from wall to wall, lay a line of dead squirrels. Squirrels with bushy tails and beady eyes. I gasped and stood back.

"Oh, they won't hurt you," he answered. "They're dead. I got 'em this evening."

I stared at him, trying to decide if he was for real.

"I hope you don't mind. I know I told you six-thirty, but it was such a wonderful evening to hunt. I couldn't get myself to leave the woods. Please forgive me. We can still catch the nine-o'clock drive-in show, if your Daddy will let you stay out a little longer."

I listened to every word, but I couldn't tear my stare from the back seat. "But what are *those*?" I asked, still pointing.

"Dead squirrels," he said again.

"I know those are dead squirrels, but what are those things hopping all around them?"

"Oh, those! Squirrel fleas." He smacked at them with an old rag, and they scattered.

"See there? They won't hurt you. They're leaving the dead bodies."

Was he crazy? Had he lost his mind, thinking I'd climb into a car with dead squirrels and squirrel fleas? Was I even crazier for considering it?

"I'm going to drop them off at Grandma's," he said, as if that explained everything. "She'll fix them tomorrow for supper. You can talk to her while I grab a quick shower."

He smacked the backseat, floor, and windows for several seconds, and smiled. Then he held the front door open wide.

I bit my lip, told myself not to look over my shoulder, and climbed inside.

We drove to David's grandparents' house, where he'd lived since he was about eleven years old. While David cleaned the squirrels, Pa and Daisy—the names David used when introducing them—made me feel at home right away. We talked and smiled, and somehow it came out in the conversation that David was supposed to have picked me up at six-thirty for the seven-o'clock movie.

David's grandfather gave him a stern look and told him never to do a girl that way. "When you tell her something, you'd better mean it. Be on time."

Daisy took the squirrels right away and soaked them in a pan of salt water.

David and I left for the late show, and we enjoyed the movie. Afterward, he asked me if I'd like to go out the next weekend, too. I really liked him and said *yes*. I was glad Daddy extended my curfew that night, because it was really late when I arrived home.

Wide awake, Daddy waited on me. "Is everything okay?" he asked.

"I'm fine. We had a good time."

He carefully scanned my face, looked hard into my eyes. "Okay," he finally said. "Lock the door and get to bed."

I washed my face, brushed my teeth, put on my pajamas and eased into bed. I drifted off quickly and dreamed that night of beady-eyed squirrels scampering in and out of the red Volkswagen.

The next week one of my teachers told me a bakery in town needed someone to work Saturdays. She thought I might be interested since she knew that I worked at the school. Since Daddy's health was declining, he was no longer able to beg on the streets. We needed the extra money the bakery job could bring in. It seemed simple. I would apply for the job, and if I got it, I would simply move Saturday's chores to Sunday. Having studied it through, on Friday after school, I held my head high and strode into the bakery and asked to speak to the manager.

A large, brown-haired woman approached me. "Hours are eight in the morning to six in the evening," she said. "Wear a white blouse, and bring a hair net."

I did. Daddy dropped me off at 7:45 the next morning. The delicious aroma of freshly baked goodies overwhelmed me. My mouth watered as I gazed at the freshly made donuts, long johns, and the assortment of cookies filling the display cases. Women in white uniforms hurried from the back, carrying large metal trays of lemon-and jelly-filled donuts. They placed them in the storefront windows and on the shelves behind the counter. Next came the trays of brownies and cupcakes. Those were placed away from the customers, near the kitchen doors.

The manager brought out a large bowl of vanilla frosting and motioned me to the back counter near the cupcakes and brownies. "Watch me," she said. She picked up a vanilla cupcake with her left hand

and swiped a slender metal spatula through the frosting with her right hand. The end of the spatula came out with about two tablespoons of fluffy white frosting. "Now, with one twist of the wrist, frost the entire top. Only turn the cupcake once," she said.

I did. Mine looked like hers, except I turned the cupcake twice. "No, you must only turn once," she said.

I tried again. I got it right that time.

She nodded, and next she showed me how to frost a large tray of brownies, by wiggling a wide metal tool to make zigzag marks on the top. She frosted a pan full, and I frosted a pan full. Mine looked identical to hers. She said so and smiled politely. She picked up a nine-inch round vanilla cake. "This cake is to be frosted like a cupcake, except you turn it twice. Hold the cake in your left hand, and the spatula in your right hand."

I did.

"For the top, dip your spatula up to four times, no more. The most important thing," she said, "is to make sure the top is completely smooth for the cake decorator."

I followed her directions, and my cake looked like hers. Again, she said so. That day, I frosted several trays of brownies, dozens of vanilla and chocolate cupcakes, and several eight- and nine-inch cakes. I paid careful attention to the samples that she left in front of me. I asked the cake decorator if my tops were smooth enough for her. She said they were fine, and the surfaces were perfect to write on. I worked hard all day, minus a couple of brief bathroom breaks and a ten-minute lunch break to eat the sandwich I'd brought from home.

Around 5:45 that evening, the workers prepared for closing. One covered the trays of unsold goodies, one swept the floor, and one wrapped the bread and rolls. The owner stood near the cash register and counted money. There were a few minutes left on the clock. I offered to help the worker wrapping the bread. She thanked me.

Six o'clock came. The workers gathered their belongings and headed for the door. I followed. The owner looked up from the cash register and called me over.

"I won't need you next week," she said, fumbling through receipts.

"Okay." I turned to leave. "I'll see you Saturday after next."

"No, I don't need you then, either. Today is all."

I scratched my cheek. "But . . . I thought I worked hard today. I—I did everything you asked."

"You did," she said. "You are a very hard worker. But you used the wrong hand."

"I don't understand."

"You used your left hand. I told you to use your right."

I held out both hands and lifted my left one. "I'm left-handed."

"Doesn't matter. Goodbye." She turned her attention back to her money, thus dismissing me.

I was hurt. This was the second time I had been told that I couldn't do something because I used the wrong hand. Not to mention that I had given up a whole day to be there and had worked *hard* all day. Why didn't she tell me my left hand was unacceptable to use when I frosted the first cupcake? I walked out where Daddy waited to take me home.

I never told him what happened, but instead pretended everything was okay. I told Daddy that I had decided the hours were too long, so I would find another Saturday job. The only time I had fibbed to him was about Mommy's letters. Well, actually I didn't fib, I didn't do what he said to do. This time, I actually fibbed, and I felt bad for doing it.

When Monday morning came, I was bothered by the fact that I had worked hard all day on Saturday and hadn't been paid. I got enough courage to speak to one of the owners who worked at the school. "Do you think you deserve payment?" she asked. I looked her square in the eye and answered, "Yes, I do. I was there all day and did everything I was asked to do." She stared at me, opened her purse and handed me a $20.00 bill.

I didn't apply for any more Saturday jobs during my junior year. I continued working daily for the teachers at school. Whenever I could, I earned extra money from the neighbors by washing their dishes, mopping, and cleaning house. They never told me I used the wrong hand and were glad to see me coming no matter what hand the scrub brush was in.

Senior Year

My senior year, 1970. Margaret was in the 8th grade and Noah in the 6th. I continued the secretarial-and-business curriculum in school. I was elected homeroom president for the third year running and served as Senior Class Secretary. I had hours of homework each night—bookkeeping, shorthand, business machines, literature, and social studies. I worked hard, kept up with my studies, and made good grades. Evenings were always busy because of the extra chores at home. Daddy wasn't doing too well and was on several medications. I again thought to be thankful we owned a car that was an automatic. He was weaker and wouldn't have been able to climb into The Goose.

I will never forget The Goose. Often, something would happen to make me think of him. When I took driver's education that year, my instructor was Willie Akers, Logan High Basketball coach. I waited patiently for my turn to drive. He took four students out at a time, and I was in the last group. I sat in the car and bobbed and jerked along with everyone else while one of the other three was driving. I was the last driver, and I couldn't wait to get my hands on the steering wheel. I got in the car, checked the mirrors, looked both ways and pulled away from the curb smooth and easy. Driving was everything I had thought it would be and more.

"My, you've driven before," Coach Akers said.

"Not from this side of the car," I said.

He looked at me and creased his forehead. But I never told him about The Blue Goose. I passed the driving and written test and received my driver's license while in the class.

All through senior year, I worked after school until 5 o'clock every day as an assistant secretary for the Board of Education. I was a secretarial floater, and I worked in all departments. The office was located in the middle of town, a block from the G.C. Murphy Co., where Daddy and I used to sell pencils. I enjoyed working at the Board of Education and learned so much from the different duties I was assigned. I worked in payroll, accounts payable, school attendance, and insurance.

The job I loved most was operating the antique switchboard with all the pull cables and levers. It looked like the one Lily Tomlin used on *Laugh-In*. Sometimes, when office staff walked by, I imitated Lily. "Hello, have I reached the party to whom I'm speaking?" Each time, they'd cackle. I came to know several teachers and principals. Interacting with them gave me a yearning to become a teacher. I wanted to become a part of their respected professional community.

In January, some of my classmates met with Mrs. McCloud, the guidance counselor, and shared some encouraging news. I learned that anyone could go to college if they had taken algebra, completed the ACT Test, had at least a 2.5 GPA, and was graduated from high school. I had completed three out of four—only a few months left until graduation. The only other requirements were a completed application to a college of choice and a declared major. And there were scholarships given out that paid all or most of the tuition and board based on your GPA, if you qualified. I couldn't believe my ears. My GPA was well above 3.00. This sounded so simple. All this time I didn't bother with it because I figured it was for students who were eights, tens, and twelves, *not for me—a one!*

The next day, I went to see Mrs. McCloud and completed an application for Marshall University in Huntington, West Virginia, along with a couple of other forms, and left them with her. My degree selected was EDUCATION. I wanted to be a teacher! I was nervous because I didn't know anything about college—where I'd live, how I would get books, or how I'd even get there. But I was excited.

A few weeks later, she called me into her office. "You've been accepted by Marshall University in Huntington, West Virginia," she said.

Before I had time to reply, she added, "Or would you rather take a work-study program at Berea College in Berea, Kentucky?"

I couldn't believe it! I had been accepted to *two* colleges! I was going to be a schoolteacher! I struggled not to cry, and I hugged my arms around myself. Finally, something good was happening to me. No, this was something *great!*

"You don't have to tell me today," she said. "Discuss it with your parents and let me know tomorrow."

All day during classes I thought about how wonderful it would be to be the one standing at the front of the classroom, teaching my own students. I could hardly wait to get home and tell Daddy.

When I stepped off the school bus that evening, I saw Daddy slouched in the porch rocker, leaning to one side. He looked old and feeble. Instantly, I changed my mind. I couldn't leave him to go away to college. Who would care for him or my brother and sister? They were twelve and fourteen, and I was all they had.

The next day, my hands trembled so much when I opened the door to the guidance counselor's office that I clasped them behind my back, lest she see. I'd already practiced what I'd say to her so the words would come out strong instead of shaky. I promised myself I wouldn't cry.

The guidance counselor frowned and her lips twisted sideways when I told her the news. She remained silent for several seconds.

"I'll ask the chairman of the business department to add your name to the list of graduating seniors seeking secretarial jobs in Logan." I nodded and went back to class.

As I entered my second semester of the school year, things improved somewhat for my family. Someone from the state came to the house and made a mold of Daddy's leg stump. They told him he qualified for a free artificial leg. He also completed papers that allowed him to receive a little extra income each month. It wasn't a great amount, but even a few extra dollars made our lives more bearable. Since Daddy's health was declining, he was not able to beg on the streets or pick berries like he used to, so every dime was needed even more.

I had so much to do my second semester. Sometimes I imagined I was on a runaway train without brakes. I faithfully kept up with housework, laundry, schoolwork, and my job at the Board of Education. I made sure to spend time helping the kids with their homework problems.

And, of course, now I made time for David. We'd dated almost two years, and I had fallen in love with him. On our weekend dates, he'd pick me up in his used 1962 Plymouth Valiant he'd recently gotten. We'd spend time watching TV and enjoying a bowl of popcorn at his grandparents' house, walking through Chief Logan State Park, or enjoying a movie at Logan Theater.

David loved the outdoors and shared his favorite hunting spots with me. We took his little beagle, Bill, and let him explore the woods with us. He was an A#1 rabbit dog. Often they would be thrashing through sage brush and briar thickets above the slate dump. Sometimes I envied Bill.

Not only was I growing closer to David, but I came to love and respect his grandparents as well. They were kind and loving and treated me like a granddaughter.

As spring neared, I encountered the extra work of preparing for graduation. I ordered my cap and gown, bought a white dress and shoes for the ceremony, and selected my graduation announcements. The guidance counselor met with me once more. She went over my GPA and graduation ranking. Normally, I would have graduated thirty-fifth out of 450 students, but since I was a class officer, my rank was seventh out of 450. I was stunned to hear this news, and happy.

My guidance counselor had more good news. She'd scheduled an interview for me in town for a possible job opportunity following graduation. I hummed all the way home. For the first time in my life, I believed things might be working out.

I still had a few more things to do prior to graduation. With the money I'd carefully budgeted and saved, I bought new clothes for my Daddy, my brother, and my sister to wear to my graduation. In one of Mommy's letters, she had written her phone number. I used my neighbor's phone, called her in Cleveland and invited her to my graduation.

Mommy declined, saying she didn't have a way to come home.

I got up the nerve to ask her what I had wanted to know for nearly four years. I spoke clearly into the receiver. "Mommy, why did you leave us?"

There was a slight pause at the other end. In a clear but serious voice, I heard, "Because I was tired of being poor and never having anything." I don't remember exactly what was said after that, but we talked a little more before we hung up.

I placed the phone on the hook and stared at it for a minute. There it was. The answer I had been waiting to hear. Poverty is cruel, but did it give her the right to walk out on us? Daddy experienced suffering and defeat along with her, *but he stayed.*

I was hurt that Mommy couldn't be there, but I knew Daddy would be. That would have to be enough. I busied myself getting ready for a day I had long been waiting for.

Graduation Day

The graduation ceremony began at ten and ended by noon. As always, the Logan High School field house was overflowing. David posed briefly for pictures with his Daddy and grandparents, and I posed for photos of Daddy and me. Afterward, David and I pulled onto the lot of Gino's Pizza across the Water Street Bridge. We celebrated our graduation with a large cheese pizza, then headed to one of David's favorite fishing holes.

About an hour later, we pulled into the parking lot of Lakeside Bait and Tackle located near Dingess, WV. "Wait here," he said.

I stayed in the car and stretched my neck to look at the blue-green water of Laurel Lake. It was a narrow body of water nestled in a peaceful valley between two steep ridgetops. On the far side of the lake, bushes of pink and white Mountain Laurel settled between a mixture of maple, oak, and birch trees. A couple of fishermen stood on the shore casting their lines into the water.

It was a warm June day in 1971, a perfect day for fishing. This was my first time. David had taken me squirrel hunting one time, but he never took me back. He said I was too noisy. He could ease up dry creek beds without rustling a leaf, and always stopped and listened before he took a step.

Not me.

I was too interested in opening a Little Debbie lunch cake or popping a stick of gum.

David now returned with two Cokes, two packages of cheese

crackers, and a pint of night crawlers. He drove us down the hill to the boat ramp, where an attendant unlocked one of the twelve-foot johnboats.

David seated himself in the middle near the oars. I sat one seat over, facing my good-looking companion. The creaking oars beat the water in unison, pulling us farther into the lake. Soon we reached the other side. David stopped rowing. The boat drifted gently, pushed by a soft summer breeze, while David's eyes surveyed something along the bank.

"What is it?" I asked.

"Come here," he said. "Sit beside me."

If I stood, I'd rock the boat. I didn't care for an impromptu swim. "I'm fine where I am."

"I want to teach you how to row."

I didn't need to know how to row. "You go ahead. You're doing a great job."

"But I need you to do this."

"Why?" I asked. "We're doing all right like this."

"Do you see that beech tree?" he asked, pointing toward the bank.

"The one that's halfway in the water?"

"Yeah. I know there's a big bass hiding in the brush under that tree. I aim to get him." He patted the seat and slid over to make room for me.

I carefully stepped from my seat to sit beside him, pleased the boat didn't capsize.

David showed me how to steady the boat by slowly maneuvering the oars back and forth in the water. After a few minutes, he moved to the other seat, picked up his fishing rod, and attached a wriggling night crawler. He stood confident and cast near the sunken tree—and a perfect cast it was. It landed close, but did not snag.

I kept the boat steady near the shoreline while he cast a few more times. Within a few minutes, something jerked hard on his line. He jerked back. The reel whizzed as the line ran. He reeled hard and fast. Soon, a large, three-pound bass broke water and struggled to free itself from the hook, then it headed for deep water. The fight was on. After five minutes of reeling hard, the bass surfaced. David pulled it closer. He plunged his hand into the water, grabbed the bass by the lips, and dropped it into the boat.

A thrill raced along my neck. I'd been a part of this catch, though only by steadying the boat. My first time fishing, my first time rowing a boat, I'd helped David catch a bass.

That night, we had fried fish for dinner. It was, no doubt, one of the best meals I'd ever tasted.

Kathy, her dad, and Margaret before graduation

Moving On

The day after graduation, David landed a job at Laura Coal and Coke Co. as an apprentice for a purchasing agent and safety director. His office was located in a small trailer not too far from the mines. An attorney in Logan hired me as a legal secretary in a one-girl office. It was located in the White & Browning Building near the top floor. I enjoyed riding the elevator and looked forward to having lunch with some of the other secretaries who worked in the building.

A little more than two months later, on a Saturday, we decided to relax by riding around, being carefree, and enjoying our freedom from school and work. Thin, transparent clouds floated overhead, and the late-summer sun warmed our skin. We turned onto Holden Road and drove to the top of the mountain.

The gate leading to the dirt road we'd planned to travel was locked. David parked the car on the edge of the road and grabbed his binoculars. We began climbing the narrow path leading to the tower. Halfway up, he pulled on a low-hanging branch of a peach tree and plucked a ripe peach from the end. He rubbed it against his shirt several times to remove the fuzz, and he handed it to me. Perfectly ripe. When I took a bite of the sweet peach flesh, juice ran down my chin.

When we reached the bottom steps of the fire tower located on top of Twenty Two Mountain in Holden, David cupped a hand around his mouth. "Hello in the tower! Anyone there?"

Nobody answered. Usually during fire season, an observer manned the tower daily, looking for forest fires. If they saw smoke, they called it in to the Department of Natural Resources in Milton, about seventy-five miles away. Sometimes observers lived year round in small cabins next to their towers. Other observers stayed during the fire seasons—March through May and October through December.

Today, the tower was vacant and silent. We paused at the foot of the steps and stared at the lookout cabin, perched about ninety feet in the air.

"Come on," David said, taking hold of my hand. "Let's climb."

"No way. That's too high." I sat down on one of the bottom steps. "You go ahead."

He gave me one of his best teasing smiles. "Come on. I'm not leaving you here at the bottom. Go halfway with me."

How could I say no to that handsome grin? "All right. I'll go halfway, but no farther."

We climbed together, step by step, side by side, resting to catch our breath on the square, wooden platforms between flights of steps. After a while, the steps narrowed, and David took the lead. I followed, and every time I hesitated, he'd again take my hand and urge me onward.

Finally, we stood on the last flight of steps, directly beneath the observation deck. David pushed on the trap door above us. It opened, and we climbed inside the stuffy six-by-six observatory. Four walls of windows looked out over the forest. We opened two of them, and a quick, rushing breeze cooled the little compartment. The beautiful, green tree canopy rustled below us.

A three-foot round table with a topography map spread across the top sat in the middle of the small room. A long, slender pointer rod ran through the center. David turned the pointer on the topography map in different directions, and he looked through his binoculars. He pointed out of one of the windows, toward the hazy mountains in the distance. "That's north," he said. "Charleston is beyond those hills."

My gaze followed his finger. "That's where I'm from. I was born in a house on Paint Creek near there." I looked around a little more. A red-tailed hawk soared effortlessly across the blue sky. "If that's north, over there's Kentucky," I said. "That's where I used to pick berries with Daddy. And over there's our Mud Fork house. I bet Daddy's rocking on the front porch right now."

David's eyes searched the mountains quietly, hardly breathing. He seemed to be listening to them. I grew quiet and did the same. A brisk wind swayed the treetops below us and whistled through the open windows. The small cabin rocked gently in the wind. Big white clouds floated overhead, so near it seemed I could almost touch them.

I could hardly believe David and I were here together, sharing this faultless day, a day unlike any other I'd ever experienced. The silence was utterly peaceful.

David's voice jarred me from my dreamlike reverie. "Will you marry me?"

This most wonderful day I'd ever lived became perfect.

"Yes, David Manley. Yes, I will marry you."

I loved David, and I knew he loved me. I looked forward to my new life with him. He was kind, a hard worker, and loved outdoor adventures like me. We would be fine.

Priorities

David and I set our wedding date for the next June, and we began making plans. I'd never felt so happy! Now that I had a job, I'd had two important things at the top of my to-do list; now with the wedding, I had three.

The first was to get a car.

Daddy drove me back and forth to work for a few weeks so I could save money for a down payment on a car. There were so many things I wanted to buy— things I really needed—but I was strict with my money those first few weeks of employment. I needed that down payment more than anything else.

Daddy was now on medication several times a day, but he still wasn't feeling all that well. I hated to bother him to drive me back and forth, so I promised myself I'd get a car as soon as possible.

Before long, my frugality paid off, and I had saved two hundred dollars. Daddy drove me to Minton Chevrolet in Logan, and we looked around the used-car lot. Daddy stopped in front of a green and white Chevy. He looked it over real good, inspecting under the hood, checking tread on the tires, and rocking the bumpers. Lastly, he thumped on the fenders. A salesman stood nearby.

"What's the lowest you can go?" Daddy asked.

"Come into the office, and we'll figure it out."

A little while later, I drove off the lot in a 1966 Chevelle Malibu. It cost eight hundred dollars, and my payments were fifty dollars a month.

"I want you to have a good-running car that will take you and bring you back," Daddy said. "I don't want you to go through all the breakdowns that I have."

I followed Daddy home in his old, smoking Ford, playing with all the buttons and controls. Everything worked. The windows rolled up and down easily, not like those in The Blue Goose. Meanwhile, my car had a radio that *actually worked!* I tuned it to WLOG, a local station, and listened to music while I drove. I tried the heater and air conditioner, too. The instrument panel and dome light lit up, unlike The Blue Goose. We'd had to shine a flashlight at night to see inside the truck. My Chevelle was clean, inside and out. I vowed to take care of the beautiful green seats and carpet.

When I got home, my brother and sister ran to meet me. "Take us for a ride, please!" It was my pleasure to drive them to Dairy Queen. They loved the *new* car.

Monday came, and I couldn't wait to drive my new car to work. I drove to Logan and turned across the Water Street Bridge that led to the parking lot on Middleburg Island. Pigeons scattered in all directions. I pulled onto the lot and stopped at the booth, like I had done all those many years ago with Daddy.

"Fifty-cents," the attendant said. I paid her and searched for a parking spot. I found one and pulled in. It was closer to the booth, not as far away as where Daddy always parked.

I walked across the bridge into town and stopped at the red light. While I waited for the light to change, I recalled an earlier time when Daddy and I stopped at that very same corner. We were going begging that day, and the frigid air chilled my bones through my thin coat. Not at all like today, a gorgeous day in hot, sunny August.

My office was located in the White and Browning Building. I worked from nine to five, Monday through Friday, and received a one-hour lunch break. The office was a one-attorney, one-secretary office. My boss proved to be a great person who was thoughtful and kind to me. Whenever business was a little slow, he'd give me a fifteen-minute afternoon break. Each time, I knew exactly where to go. I'd hurry to G.C. Murphy's candy counter and order a quarter pound of chocolate stars. I'd watch the clerk scoop them, weigh them, and pour them into a white paper bag, like I had imagined her doing when I was much younger.

Lunchtime was special. Down the street from where Daddy and I had begged years ago stood Franklin's, a favorite lunch counter for many people in Logan. For years, I'd dreamed of going in there to order one of their famous ham salad sandwiches. Now, a few times a week, I met a couple of other secretaries there for lunch. Franklin's was always crowded, and people stood along the wall waiting for an empty stool or booth. It proved to be worth every minute of the wait.

I earned seventy-five dollars a week—almost as much as Daddy had received in a month to feed a family of five—and I used part of the money to help my family by painting and wallpapering our house. I bought snacks for my brother and sister. I saved a little for the wedding, and I carefully shopped for bargains at local department stores. I didn't have a hope chest or trunk like other girls, but I stored my towels, sheets, and bowls in boxes. I stood my new ironing board in the corner of the bedroom, and I admired it each day when I awoke.

The second thing on my priority list was to deal with those pesky roaches that had been a part of our family since we moved in. After buying my car, I used money from my next payday to hire a professional exterminator. When I mentioned my intention to Daddy, he didn't like the idea.

"Don't go wasting your money. That spray doesn't work. Roaches have been around for thousands of years, and they can live anywhere."

"This is a different kind of spray," I said. "It's professional. We need to give it a try."

Browning Exterminators arrived early the next morning. I explained to Mr. Browning about the roach problem we'd had for the last thirteen years, since the first day we'd moved into the house. I followed him from room to room while he looked around.

Daddy never said a word.

Mr. Browning returned to his truck briefly and came back with a large silver canister. "This'll do it." He pumped the handle on it hard several times. "I'll do the outside first. You pull out all drawers in the kitchen and bedrooms."

I did. I opened all doors and windows to let out the fumes and went outside to watch. Daddy waited on the porch while Mr. Browning sprayed all windows, doorframes, porches, steps, and under the house. He sprayed the yard alongside the house. Next, he stood on a small ladder and sprayed the edge of the roof.

After what seemed like an hour, he went inside. He spent several minutes in each room, spraying carefully and heavily. Before he finished, roaches emerged slowly from their hiding places. They ran a short distance and stopped dead in their tracks. Others kicked for a while and became still.

"I've never seen them do that before," Daddy said.

"I told you, this stuff'll kill 'em," Mr. Browning said. He sprayed corners, ceilings, baseboards, under the linoleum rugs, and inside of all the furniture. He gave every room a good dousing. Dead roaches lay everywhere.

Mr. Browning stood on the porch and wrote in a little pad. He handed me a bill for twenty-five dollars. I paid him and thanked him.

"Trust me," he said. "This'll be the end of the roaches."

After he left, the four of us worked late into the evening sweeping up the dead roaches and throwing them into the burn barrel. We mopped every room and washed everything in sight. At first, it was hard to convince Daddy that Mr. Browning's spray would work. Daddy knew that roaches roamed the kitchen at night, and for the first few nights, he'd sneak into the kitchen after dark and turn on the overhead light. Not a roach in sight. Daddy searched all around the kitchen. He even opened up the kitchen cabinet and checked in the refrigerator. Nothing.

I'll never forgot Mr. Browning, or the extra kindness he showed us that day. He told the truth: we never again saw another roach. To this day, I believe it was his refilling that canister several times that did the trick. The disappearance of the roaches was an absolute blessing. We no longer had to throw out food because the roaches had found it. We no longer had to shake our clothes before we dressed in the mornings.

Now that I had a car, I was able to do more to help my family. I had a telephone installed, shopped for groceries, and took my brother and sister on errands. Daddy didn't have to struggle as much. The old blue Ford had almost seen its last days. It burned oil and smoked terribly, as Daddy wasn't physically able to keep up with the repairs. I knew that soon it would end up in the salvage yard where The Blue Goose was taken.

Several months after Daddy had traded The Goose, our school bus took an alternate road home due to road repairs on my normal route. This road passed by the salvage yard, and when the flagman signaled the bus driver to stop, I glanced beyond the fence to the huge piles of automobile parts unknown to me. In their midst were huge piles of scrap iron and junked cars with broken windshields.

In this iron graveyard, I spotted The Blue Goose parked beside the other junked cars, her hood high in the air, minus The Goose hood ornament. She was almost unrecognizable as she had been dismantled piece by piece. Almost completely stripped, she rested on the ground. There was only a trace of the faded blue paint left. The interior was gutted; all that remained was the steering and stick shift that worked when I rode with Daddy years ago. I suddenly longed for one more ride in The Goose with Daddy sitting by my side. The Goose gave our family all she had, and even in the junkyard she benefited others with her few precious parts.

The flagman signaled us through, and the bus jerked along when the driver changed gears. I kept looking in the direction of The Goose. I felt regret that I had wished her gone, although I knew Daddy wasn't able to keep her running any longer. I would always remember our trips to town with Mommy. For a second I saw her sitting up front with a red and black flowered head scarf tied tight under her chin. She held out a small white bag from the dime store. "Here's a chocolate star," she said. "Just take one."

After all these years, it seemed like things were beginning to look up for our family. That is, our family minus Mommy. Mommy still lived in Cleveland. We talked occasionally, but she never mentioned coming back home. When Margaret and Noah spoke to her, it was the same conversation. "Hi. What are you doing? Nothing. Well, here's Noah." They handed the phone back and forth. It was almost as if they didn't know her, or they were talking to someone they had just met.

One thing I was relieved to know, something that had been my dark fear. I wasn't the reason that Mommy left.

Engagement

Summer turned into fall, and too soon, we found ourselves dealing with winter again. Same cold temperatures and snow but then winter sneaked in a long, hard rain.

Friday, February 26, 1972, arrived, along with more rain. Rain had poured all week, and our creek was swollen. Fridays were date nights for David and me, but tonight I was concerned about flooding. I called David. "Are we still going out? The underpass might be flooded."

"We'll be all right. Only a little mountain run-off up my way." He picked me up minutes later, and we headed to the movies. The Mud Fork underpass was partially blocked when we drove by. "It'll be okay," he said. "I've seen it like this before."

The movie ended. We left the theater in a torrential downpour. Water ran across the sidewalks, down the streets, and toward the overflowing drains. By the time we reached the car, we were soaked to the skin. We had planned to go for pizza but thought it best to head home. Sure enough, the road leading to my house was blocked. David turned the car around and drove to his grandparents' house where I spent the night with Pa and Daisy.

David and I shared a homemade Chef Boy-Ar-Dee pizza, while listening to the *Top Twenty Countdown*. Harry Nilsson sang "Without You," as David handed me a small, white box.

My fingers trembled as I opened it. Inside, a small diamond glittered atop a gold engagement ring. Happy tears sprang to my eyes.

The next morning, David's grandparents rose early. Gravy and biscuits waited for David and me when we awoke. Pa and Daisy were overjoyed with our engagement news, and they generously offered to let us rent the small, two-story apartment behind their house.

After breakfast, they showed us around. On the bottom floor was a small kitchen with a cinderblock laundry and storage room on the other side. Steps led to the second floor where a small bathroom sat at the end of an L-shaped room which easily could be divided into a living room and bedroom.

"Fix it up however you like," Daisy said.

Thrilled at the little house's potential, I squeezed David's hand to let him know I wanted it. David accepted his grandparents' kind offer, and we headed back to their house in the continuing rain.

I put a hand to my mouth when I saw that the shallow creek across the road from the house now roared and threatened to climb out of her bed. "Would you look at that!"

"It's probably flooding somewhere," Pa said. "Let's get inside, and I'll turn on the news." We hurried inside, and Pa turned on the radio and adjusted the dial. Instead of hearing the usual news coverage, we heard a frantic voice.

"Get away from the river!" the newscaster warned. "A dam has broken. A wall of water is headed downriver. The debris is knocking out bridges." He grabbed a breath. "Several people have been swept away."

Without realizing it, we had awakened to the most horrific tragedy that had ever unfolded in Logan County. The Buffalo Creek Dam, a slurry impoundment at Pittston Coal Company in Man, West Virginia, had burst, spilling over 132 million gallons of black sludge water over the sixteen coal camps downstream.

Throughout the day, we listened to updates. Entire communities washed away, and many people were dead or missing. Late that night, David drove through the partially blocked Mud Fork underpass and took me home. Over the next few days, updates kept pouring in. One-hundred-twenty-six people were killed, eleven hundred more were injured, and over four thousand were left homeless.

This devastating news dampened my spirits, and I felt the need to hear my mother's voice. I called her at her home in Cleveland. We discussed the Buffalo Creek disaster, and I told her I was engaged.

"That's good news," she said. "I'm happy for you."

Five years had passed since that brisk October day when she'd left. I invited her to the wedding, but, again, she said she wouldn't have a way to come home. I was disappointed, but I had accepted that she had made another life for herself and we, her family, were not included. I wondered why she still called and wrote letters.

Fortunately, my days were packed so full of busyness that I had no time to stress over the fact that Mommy couldn't attend my wedding. After working all day, I'd come home, cook, and clean. Daddy's health continued to decline. Now sixty-one years old, his hand stayed numb, and it was difficult for him to hold onto even the lightest pots or pans. He struggled to cook or wash dishes. He walked more slowly now, too.

My brother spent most of his time in the woods or hanging out with friends. My sister helped as much as she could, but she was often busy with homework, and she spent time with her boyfriend. I didn't begrudge the kids these breaks from chores, as I wanted so much for them to have an easier time of things than I'd had at their ages.

During any spare time, I worked to get our little apartment ready. Our June eighth wedding day would soon arrive, and I yearned for David and me to have a pretty home in which to begin our married life together. David and I worked on the house every weekend during March and April, cleaning and painting the small rooms. We scrubbed the windows and floors. We hung curtains. By the end of May, we were ready to move in furniture.

It pleased us to find good used furniture. Pa and Daisy gave us an old white wooden bed, and we bought a small chest. That completed our tiny bedroom. We purchased a used green sofa and a red velvety chair. The colors didn't go together, but it didn't matter to us, because we covered them with blue-flowered throws from the dime store, and we hung blue curtains to match. David moved in his brown wooden desk and chair. We had a coffee table, an end table, and a lamp. A Philco TV completed our first living room.

The kitchen came last. We bought a used kitchen table with a green Formica top and four matching chairs. We found a good, used gas range and refrigerator, but we purchased a new double-bowl sink. One small kitchen cabinet stored our dishes, pots, and pans. A large gas heater stood beside the range. That heater was our only source of warmth for the whole apartment. David and I purchased a small window air conditioner, and we put it upstairs. I couldn't imagine the luxury of having an air conditioner. We only had a window fan back home.

David and I stood back and admired the rooms as we finished each one. We had a green-and-gold kitchen, a blue living room, and a pink bedroom. Finally, I had the pink bedroom I had always dreamed about—the one I'd asked God for a few years ago. Though other men might have fussed over a pink bedroom, David didn't mind. If it made me happy, he was happy.

There was one more thing we did to make our home completely comfortable. The house had settled backward about four inches on its foundation. As a result, we had to scotch the furniture with small wedges of wood to make each piece sit level. When we were moving in, we thought we were finished scotching all the furniture, and we went upstairs to take a break. As soon as we sat down on the sofa, the TV slid away from the wall and came halfway across the room toward us. We recovered from the shock, had a good laugh, and put in more scotchies!

Daddy smiled each time I talked about getting married. He'd grown fond of David. I worried more about Daddy's health, and though I could hardly wait to marry my sweetheart, I could barely think of leaving Daddy and the kids without my heart breaking. The house David and I would share was twenty minutes away from my family. Each time I left, it felt like that distance grew.

A few days before David and I were to be married, we moved our clothes and other personal items into the apartment. I emptied my metal cabinet in the bedroom and found a small box with a few Mallo Cup cards. I smiled. Although I never did get the 500 points needed to send in for a box of candy, I remembered the times I spent checking around the garbage can at the Island Creek Store and asking kids for them at school. It was a childhood dream that gave me hope. I removed one from the box and rubbed the small cardboard between my fingers. MALLO CUP PLAY MONEY the card said. STICK ON TAPE—AVOID DELAY. I dropped the card into the box and threw it in the trash. Those days were long gone. My Big Ben statue, with an unpainted tie, rested on top of my cabinet, and that's where I left it. I wanted Daddy to have something to help him not feel so lonely.

I dreamed of cooking our first meal as I organized the kitchen in our new house. David drove me back to Daddy's for one last small load, and when we pulled near the house, a neighbor sat on the porch beside Daddy, flagging me to hurry.

Concern etched her face. "A few minutes ago," she said as I neared the porch, "he stumbled out here and slumped into this chair. He never did change position, so I hollered and asked if he was okay."

"Daddy," I said, kneeling in front of him. "What's wrong?"

He didn't respond.

I rushed him to the hospital. His blood pressure was high, and he didn't remember if he'd taken his medicine that morning.

The doctor worked with him for a while before he handed me Daddy's prescriptions. "He needs to take better care of himself. This was bad, but it could have been worse."

I could read between the lines. I stayed with Daddy and cared for him until he got better. I told him what the doctor had said. "Daddy, you need to cut down on fried foods and sugary things. The doctor said this is what's making you feel so bad all the time."

Daddy's expression looked as though he'd been smacked. "I've been eating this way all of my life, Kathy. It's too hard to quit now." After much coaxing, Daddy tried to cut back on the greasier foods he ate, but he refused to give up bacon and eggs.

Daddy disliked telephones and never liked to talk on one. I spent the afternoon teaching him how to dial my work number and how to call me at my new home. I called him every morning and afternoon from work. I could tell by the way he answered the phone if he was okay or not. If he didn't answer, or if his speech wasn't clear, I immediately went to check on him.

Nothing made me happier than to know I'd be living with David in our new home, but leaving reminded me of the day when Mommy left. Though I knew my moving out was under much different circumstances, I felt that I was walking out the door on Daddy, my brother, and my sister like Mommy had done.

Wedding Day

I hurried to the kitchen and turned off the eight o'clock alarm. It was our only clock, our Big Ben. Daddy had placed it on top of the refrigerator, and that's where it stayed.

"Keep it in the kitchen," Daddy said. "That way, we can hear it when it goes off. No one will be going back to sleep if we have to get out of bed to turn it off."

Often I was still drowsy when I reached the kitchen to turn off the alarm. This morning, I was wide awake. I didn't think once about going back to bed for five more minutes, as I usually did. I couldn't afford to linger in bed one extra second.

Daddy had heard the alarm, too, and he sat up in bed. Unbelievably, my brother and sister did not even stir. School had been out for a week or so, and they enjoyed sleeping in, so I let them.

I quickly dressed and rolled my hair on large plastic rollers. Daddy puttered in the kitchen, filling his whistling teakettle. He loved his morning cup of instant coffee.

I grabbed the bottles of ginger ale we'd need for our reception, and I headed toward the door. "Bye, Daddy. I'll be back in time to help get everybody ready."

Daddy met me halfway, carrying a bag of mints, assorted nuts, and wedding napkins.

"Be careful," he said, loading the bag into my arms. He waved goodbye and shut the door behind me.

I had only been to one wedding, and that was two months earlier. Debbie got married, and I was one of her bridesmaids. I learned how to plan a wedding from listening to Debbie and her mother. After she married, she moved to Kentucky, so I no longer had her help. I missed her terribly. She and I had been close friends since the sixth grade, and we had talked almost every day either sitting on her porch or my back steps.

David and his best man left for Charleston to pick up their wedding attire. There'd been a problem with the first tuxedo measurement, so they made the trip again in my Chevelle. I don't remember why they didn't drive one of their vehicles, but I was happy to let them borrow mine. David would have the car back to me before I headed to the church. Someone would follow him to my house and take him back home.

I spread clean sheets over the car seats and in the trunk of Daddy's old blue Ford before I headed out to run errands. I crossed my fingers and hoped the Ford wouldn't backfire while I was driving through town and that it wouldn't smoke so much.

My first stop was the flower shop in Logan. Luckily, I found a parking space not too far from the door. I saved money by picking up the candleholders, flower stands, and candelabra myself, as they charged an extra delivery fee to take them to the church and pick them up after the ceremony. I lifted the box holding my wedding bouquet, the corsages, and the boutonnières.

"I love your choice of colors," the clerk said. "Aqua and coral go so well together."

"Thank you."

I chose those colors because the fabric was on sale when I purchased the patterns for the bridesmaid and maid of honor, but I never mentioned that to her. I saved money by having my wedding veil and the dresses made, and I only paid $30.00 for my wedding gown from J. C. Penney. I had carefully budgeted everything for the wedding including food for our reception. It took me three trips to get everything loaded because she was the only one in the shop that day and couldn't help me.

My next stop was Nu-Era Bakery. Years ago, when Daddy and I came to Logan to sell pencils, I dreamed of going in there and buying one of their delicious-looking glazed donuts. Today, my chest swelled with pride when I walked in the door to purchase my wedding cake. I gently placed the three-tier cake on a bed sheet I had spread on the car's front floorboard. I didn't want to worry about it falling off the seat.

Next, I headed to Kroger to buy a few containers of lime sherbet. I picked up an extra packet of dinner mints, just in case, and I headed to Central United Baptist Church where Pa and Daisy were members.

I carried in the sherbet first and stored it in the freezer. Next, I carried in the cake and set it on the counter. I spread a tablecloth on the table and placed the bags of mints and nuts beside the cake. A couple of Daisy's friends from the church had volunteered to make the punch and serve our cake that evening for the wedding.

Finally, I carried in the items from the flower shop. I assembled the candelabra and placed it up front in the center of the church, added candles and bows, and placed a white flower stand on the sides. I walked to the back of the church and appraised the decorations. I crossed my arms, tilted my head, and rocked back on my heels. If it had been any wider, my smile would have split my cheeks.

I checked my watch and realized I had no more time to gloat. With my morning errands over, I had only enough time to hurry home and get myself—and everyone else—ready. Lucky for me, the Ford never smoked or backfired!

David parked the Chevelle in front of the house as promised. My brother met me at the door. "We made seventy-five rice bags." He held several in his hands.

I inspected a couple. "Good job! I like how you used both the aqua and coral ribbons." I'd envisioned only one or the other on each rice bag, but these looked even prettier. "Thanks!"

For an hour or more, time flew past. My brother dressed and waited for the rest of us on the front porch. My sister was ready several minutes after him. She pranced through the house, waving her arms in grand gestures, thrilled to be my only bridesmaid. My cousin Judy from Lenore was my maid of honor.

Now I helped Daddy. He wore a new jacket, shirt, and pants. He surprised me when he motioned toward his artificial leg. He'd worn it only one other time, and that was for my high-school graduation. He'd had it for about two years now, but he never wore it, because each time, it rubbed a raw place around his knee, which took several days to heal.

Once everyone else had dressed and was ready, it was my turn.

I took a quick bath, applied makeup and removed the large curlers I'd worn all morning. I grabbed my veil and my wedding gown, and I headed for the car.

"Hey, you forgot this." My sister stood on the porch, holding up my suitcase. I took it from her, and we hugged. She squeezed me tightly, and I found it hard to let her go.

Daddy and the kids would arrive a little later in the Ford. David and I needed the Chevelle for our honeymoon, so I drove. He and I arrived about the same time at the church for our pre-wedding photographs. We had carefully budgeted our wedding expenses, and we agreed to purchase a small wedding album. I hurried upstairs to change and meet the photographer. After getting the equipment ready, the photographer led me to a stained-glass window.

"Stand here," she said, and she left the room. I waited for a few minutes, thinking she went to get more film, but the door opened again. She stood beside Daddy. My breath hitched. I wasn't expecting to see him upstairs. *How did he get up all those steps?* I thought the first time we'd see each other was when I was ready to walk down the aisle. He had not seen my wedding dress.

The photographer took Daddy by the hand and led him to the window. He moved slowly supported with a cane. She positioned us so that we faced each other, and she pushed us closer together.

"I want you to look at each other," she said. She lifted my right hand and placed it on Daddy's cheek. She put my left hand on his shoulder.

I stared into Daddy's pale blue eyes, and he stared into mine. I never remembered a time when we were both so still.

"Don't say anything," she said. "Keep looking."

Daddy gazed into my eyes. I gazed into his.

If I could have talked right then, if the photographer had let me speak, I would have whispered my thoughts aloud. I teared up as my mind gathered the words:

Daddy,

Your little berry picker has grown up and is getting married today, but I'll still be around to take care of you.

I'll always remember the sounds of you strapping on your peg leg, tightening your belts and going to work for us every day. You worked so hard to raise us, and I'll always be proud of you.

Thank you for staying with us when Mommy left. You could have left too, but you didn't.

I love you so much, and I'll never forget the lessons I learned riding in The Blue Goose. Those days were the best. I can still hear you say, "See that vanilla moon? It's gonna follow us all the way home."

And about Big Ben...I'm going to England one day and see it for myself, like you urged me to do. You helped me dream, Daddy, until I could do it on my own.

Kathy and her dad on her wedding day

Nothing Remains the Same

Two months after our wedding, David and I bought a new Volkswagen. I gave the Chevelle to Daddy, and he sold his old Ford for scrap. He was so proud of that car. It was the first *new* car he'd ever owned, although it was nearly seven years old. I remember him saying, "That's the best car I've ever had. It starts every time I turn the key. I'll never have to work under that hood!"

I went to see Daddy every day either during lunch or after work. I took him lunch, helped Margaret clean house, bought groceries, and did their laundry at the laundromat. I did this up until the time of his death, four years after I was married. By then, David and I had bought a new home which had extra bedrooms for Margaret and Noah. They lived with us until Margaret got married a few months later, and Noah moved to Cleveland to be with Mom. He was starting to get in trouble at school, and I was too young to help him. After speaking to Mom on the phone, she suggested he come and live with her.

Daddy never lived to see his six grandchildren—three each from Margaret and me. He died from complications of pneumonia at sixty-four. I made the funeral arrangements and buried him.

For nearly eight years after Daddy died, I continued to work in various business positions in Logan. In December 1983, I graduated from Marshall University with a teaching degree and was hired and placed by the Logan County Board of Education. Finally, at the age of thirty-one, I had realized my dream of becoming a teacher. I was so excited and couldn't wait to start teaching my 5th grade class. They were so young, and I thought maybe I could do or say something that could help them deal with their own poverty.

After teaching for one week, Mommy called me. She had been diagnosed with ovarian cancer and wanted to come home to die. My sister wasn't working at the time and went to Cleveland, brought her home and cared for her for the next few weeks until she died. Before she passed away at the age of fifty-three, she asked to be buried beside Daddy because he was the only man who had ever loved her. She got her request. The cemetery is a fifteen-minute drive, and I place flowers on their graves twice a year.

I often wondered about their marriage and the nineteen-year age difference. Did that play a part in her leaving, or was it because living in poverty was sucking the life out of her? If so, she left while she had a little bit of life remaining in her. I had decided several years back to work hard and run from poverty. But the truth is, it wasn't just running; it was also burying your life into work so you did not have to think of it.

Kathy, her two daughters, flanking mom Rosie

Kathy's house in Verdunville ca. 2008–2010

Big Ben

Several years later, I found myself going for another exciting ride, but this time, it wasn't in The Blue Goose. I boarded Virgin Flight 11, a spacious 450-seat jetliner, headed to Europe with twenty-five of my students on board. Instead of two bucket seats with a stick shift in between, I sat by the window in a row of ten seats, surrounded by my students. They were seated in front, in back, and beside me.

They fidgeted in their seats and examined their new surroundings. They explored the headphones, the armrest radios, and the seatback TVs. They placed stickers from the courtesy bag—such as "Wake Me for Snacks," "Wake Me for Meals," and "Wake Me 30 Minutes Prior to Landing"—in various places, including the front of their shirts and on their foreheads. We fastened our seatbelts as the British pilot strolled down the aisle, leaned over, and welcomed aboard *the teacher and her students from the states.*

Our takeoff, even in the night sky, proved gorgeous, and I found myself flying over blue-black water underneath a silvery moon whose light glistened against huge puffy clouds. After a while, my students stopped fidgeting and concentrated on whatever their headphones emitted. Some drifted off to sleep after being reminded that our ten-day tour began immediately once we touched down the next morning. I put on my headphones and tuned the radio. The Beatles came through crystal clear, singing "Yesterday." I recalled our Coal Camp Beatles from so long ago, and the dream of a twelve-year-old girl and her dime.

As the plane soared above the Atlantic, I too, dozed. When I closed my eyes, I envisioned myself running through dirt-covered alleys playing with my brother and sister. Large blackberry patches filled my mind, and that huge pile of coal again loomed beside our two-room shack. My mother strummed her guitar on the front porch as we waited for an approaching thunderstorm.

The lights above our heads came on, and a stewardess stopped by to pass out mid-flight snacks. My drowsy students reached for ice cream, then settled back under their blankets, half-awake, half-eating. I remembered that long-ago day at the Dairy Freeze, and how patiently I had waited for my turn. I'd held tight to that nickel.

Sometime later, someone beside me turned on the TV, reminding me of that busy night of homework when Dad called me into the living room to watch the news and get a glimpse of Big Ben. I dozed again.

Soon we landed in London and boarded a bus to begin our first tour. As the bus cut its way through crowded streets, my students and I marveled at the majestic buildings and magnificent statues. We stopped near a stone wall in front of the Thames River to take pictures. Our tour guide ushered everyone off the bus and led us to a railing. I didn't follow. Instead, I lingered near a small tree and beheld the spectacle that stood before me across the river. High above the north end of the Palace of Westminster stood a 315-foot tower with a four-faced clock. This was the same icon I'd remembered seeing on the 6:30 nightly news so long ago.

My hands trembled, and I held my breath to steady myself as I lifted my camera and snapped a picture of Big Ben. After all these years, after all these experiences, Big Ben stood tall in front of me. The tiny "Big Ben"—the Roosevelt clock I'd been so sure was Big Ben—had quit running long ago. But the dreams it had inspired still lived.

I closed my eyes tightly. "Yes, Daddy," I whispered. "He's real."

Back on the bus, I wondered for a moment how many people find something they treasure and hold on to simply because of the way it looks, feels, or what it means to them. That one special thing can help you dream, keep you moving, or motivate you to keep on when the odds are against you. Although Big Ben is one of London's best-known landmarks, he was more than that to me. When I boarded Virgin 11, I never realized the emotion I'd feel or the impact that seeing that clock would have on me. When I found Big Ben in the dump, I clung to him because he was a new-found toy, and he was mine. He represented a special place that Daddy told me was real and suggested I go see it. I wanted to see it, and I lived to see it.

The Real Big Ben

EPILOGUE

Fingertips

Recently, I applied for a substitute teaching position in my county. As a matter of routine, I had to complete a background check, and one of the requirements was to get fingerprinted. The technician could not get the four fingers on my right hand to print, so she asked me to rub lotion on them. This scenario continued about seven times—her placing my fingertips on the screen, pressing the button, not getting a desired result, then using more lotion.

Finally she asked, "Did you have your hands in bleach today?"

"Yes. Two-three drops in my dishwater this morning."

She grabbed the bottle of lotion, pumped more onto the right hand, and tried again. Same results as before. This time she called the supervisor, who tried a few times but got no results.

Next, they had me to place my fingers lightly on the screen, then press hard on the screen, then whole fingers, then roll the fingers, and last to do fingertips again. No change.

I was becoming a little upset because I could see the prints on the screen, and on the fifteenth attempt I said, "There they are. I see them. I pointed to the lines. "Those are my fingerprints."

The supervisor set the lotion back on the table. "That's not what we're looking for. Those are cracks and lines from dry fingertips. You don't have any."

I was stunned. "But even the cracks should be enough to identify my fingers," I said.

"How often do you use bleach?" she asked.

"I've cleaned and scrubbed with it all my life," I said. "Since I was about ten or twelve."

"That's why," she said. "You've worn off the whorls and loops from your fingertips due to excessive exposure."

She pointed to the fingers on the left hand. "See here. You still have whorls and loops on this hand."

I paused for a second to take in what she was saying. Although I'm left-handed, I scrubbed with my right.

Her words brought me back. "I'm not sure how this will work out for your employer, but you need to tell them. They will advise you."

I left the office feeling disappointed, but then it occurred to me later that evening that more or less I had had a "scrub brush in that hand" all my life. I pondered on it all evening because I couldn't let it go. Something kept gnawing at me, and I found myself reliving life events like someone does when they are trying to make a major decision.

I began asking myself questions. *Why am I like I am? Always working? Why am I so driven to work? Something is the cause, but this requires more thought.* I let it go for a few hours but returned right back to the discussion in my mind. *Why have I plowed through every decade of my life with a full agenda?* After giving it considerable thought, I believe I came up with the answer.

Running from poverty had driven me to work hard, to seek a higher education, and to take all the extra jobs I could to make sure that my family and I would never experience that painful life again. I was determined to break the cycle of poverty that had plagued my ancestors and maintain a comfortable level of living.

The next morning, I tossed potatoes into the sink and rinsed them before peeling them. I remembered her words: "You've worn off your fingertips due to years of frequent use of water and cleaning."

Her words still bothered me after breakfast, and I couldn't shake it. I still grabbed paper and pencil, wrote my to-do list, then headed to the laundry room. I reached into the basket to begin a load of towels, and then hesitated. I sat the basket down and plopped down in the recliner. I straightened my shoulders and breathed deeply.

It slowly unfolded. I came to understand that my sense of service and duty that compelled me to grow up so fast had remained a strong marker throughout my life. I had always been in service to somebody or something. When does it end? Who can make it stop?

Fifteen minutes later, I found myself on the front porch swing. I had a fresh cup of steaming coffee and a new book that had been sitting on my coffee table for a few months. I set the coffee on a nearby table and turned to page one. Before reading the first word, I looked beyond the banisters to the beautiful green landscape and thought...

I give myself permission to rest today.

I give myself permission to say NO.

I do not have to run from poverty anymore.

AUTHOR BIO

Katherine Manley lives in southern West Virginia and has been an educator in Logan County schools for over 35 years. Earning degrees from Marshall University and West Virginia State University, she is a National Board Certified Teacher. She is a fellow of the 1995 West Virginia Writing Project directed by Dr. Fran Simone and the 1996 West Virginia Humanities Council Appalachian Seminar directed by Dr. Judy Byers. Her writing has been featured in *Hamilton Stone Review, Traditions: A Journal of West Virginia Folk Culture and Educational Awareness, The Guyandot Observer, and Fearless: Women's Journeys to Self-Empowerment.* Her short stories have placed in West Virginia Writers' Contests, and her memoir was a semi-finalist in William Faulkner's Writing Competition. Katherine has won several prestigious teaching awards including finalist for West Virginia Teacher of the Year, Arch Coal Teacher of the Year, and The Prodigy Foundation Teacher Achievement Award given in memory of the Rocket Boys' beloved teacher, Freida J. Riley of Coalwood, West Virginia. She is married and the mother of three adult children and has two precious grandsons. In her spare time, you'll find Katherine hiking the heavenly mountains of West Virginia, reading by a cozy fire, or relaxing at the beach, taking a well-earned rest.

Made in the USA
Middletown, DE
15 July 2021